DK EYEWITNESS TOP 10 TRAVEL GUIDES

NAPLES
& THE AMALFI COAST

JEFFREY KENNEDY

DK
WWW.DK.COM

Left **Capodimonte** Right **Pompeii**

DK

LONDON, NEW YORK,
MELBOURNE, MUNICH AND DELHI
www.dk.com

Produced by Sargasso Media Ltd, London

Reproduced by Colourscan, Singapore
Printed and bound in Italy by Graphicom

First American Edition, 2004
03 04 05 06 10 9 8 7 6 5 4 3 2 1

Published in the United States by
DK Publishing, Inc.,
375 Hudson Street, New York,
New York 10014

ISSN 1479-344X
ISBN 0-7566 02912

Within each Top 10 list in this book, no hierarchy of quality or popularity is implied. All 10 are, in the editor's opinion, of roughly equal merit.

Floors are referred to throughout in accordance with Italian usage; ie the "first floor" is the floor above ground level.

See our complete product line at **www.dk.com**

Contents

Naples & The Amalfi Coast's Top 10

Highlights 6
Palazzo Reale, Naples 8
Castel Nuovo, Naples 10
Duomo, Naples 12
Museo Archeologico Nazionale, Naples 14
Capodimonte 18
Certosa di San Martino 20
Pompeii 24
Capri 28
Ravello 30
Paestum 32
Moments in History 34
Epochs and Eras 36
Museums and Galleries 38

The information in this DK Eyewitness Top 10 Travel Guide is checked regularly.

Every effort has been made to ensure that this book is as up-to-date as possible at the time of going to press. Some details, however, such as telephone numbers, opening hours, prices, gallery hanging arrangements and travel information are liable to change. The publishers cannot accept responsibility for any consequences arising from the use of this book, nor for any material on third party websites, and cannot guarantee that any website address in this book will be a suitable source of travel information. We value the views and suggestions of our readers very highly. Please write to: Publisher, DK Eyewitness Travel Guides, Dorling Kindersley, 80 Strand, London WC2R 0RL, Great Britain.

Left **Capri** Centre **Limoncello liqueur** Right **Paestum**

Churches in Naples 40

Piazzas and Fountains 42

Artists and their Masterpieces 44

Icons of Popular Culture 46

Walks 48

Beaches 50

Romantic Spots 52

Hidden Attractions 54

Children's Attractions 56

Sporting Activities 58

Neapolitan Dishes 60

Neapolitan Souvenirs 62

Religious Celebrations 64

Around Naples & The Amalfi Coast

Naples: Spaccanapoli to Capodimonte 68

Naples: Toledo to Chiaia 80

Vesuvius & Around 88

The Islands, Sorrento & the South 94

Posillipo, Pozzuoli & the North 108

Streetsmart

Practical Information 116

Places to Stay 125

General Index 134

Left **Sorrento** Right **Naples market**

Key to abbreviations
Adm *admission charge* **Free** *no admission charge* **Dis. access** *disabled access*

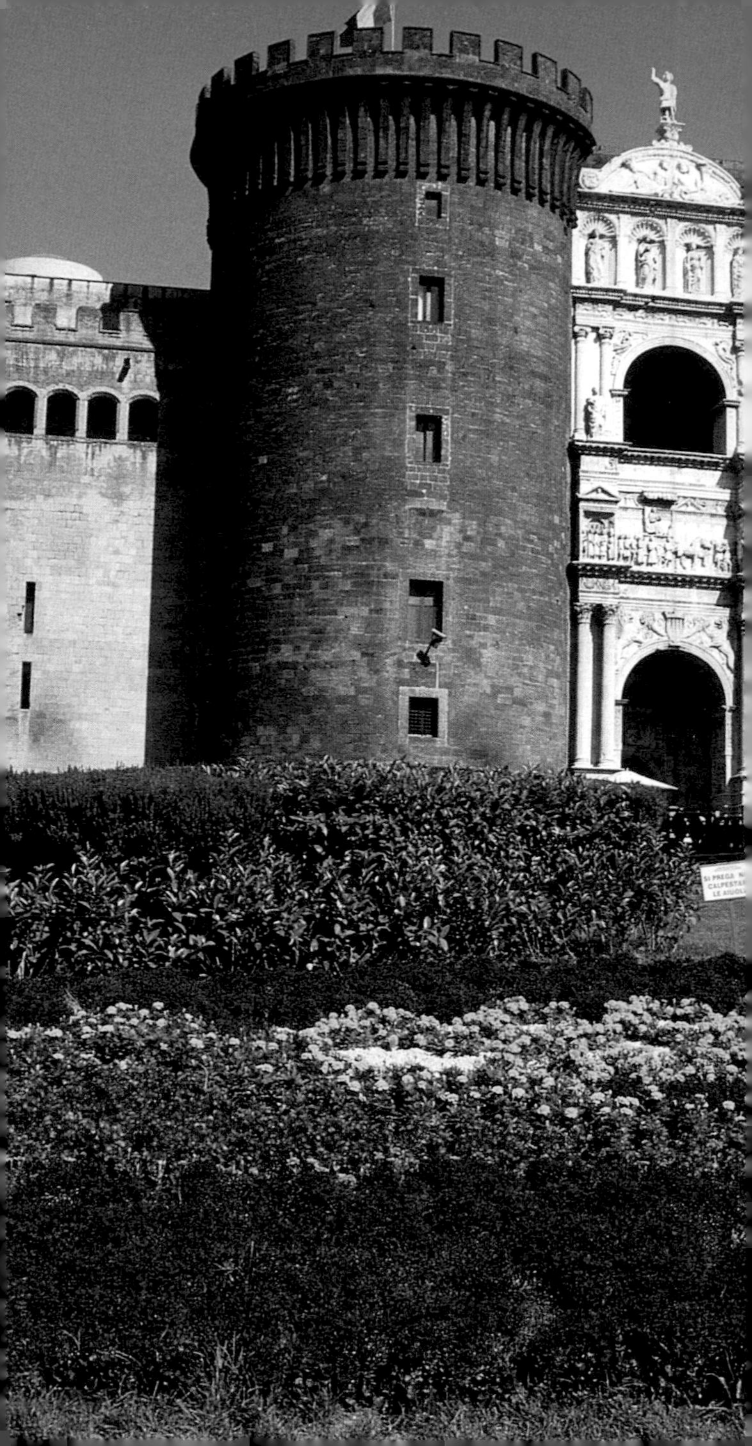
SI PREGA

NAPLES & THE AMALFI COAST'S TOP 10

Naples & the Amalfi Coast's Highlights 6–7

Palazzo Reale 8–9

Castel Nuovo 10–11

Duomo 12–13

Museo Archeologico Nazionale 14–17

Capodimonte 18–19

Certosa di San Martino 20–23

Pompeii 24–27

Capri 28–29

Ravello 30–31

Paestum 32–33

Top Ten of Everything 34–65

NAPLES & THE AMALFI COAST'S TOP 10

TOP 10 Naples & the Amalfi Coast's Highlights

From one perspective, this area is an anomaly, at once one of the earth's most beautiful and yet most accursed places. It has been the choice of the great and wealthy as their playground, while also being the scene of some of the greatest natural disasters and the grittiest human misery. Perhaps these irreconcilable twists of fate are at the root of the Neapolitans' famously optimistic cynicism. The city of Naples itself is a vibrant urban setting, almost non-European in its intensity, while the beauty of the surrounding coast has been known to make grown men weep.

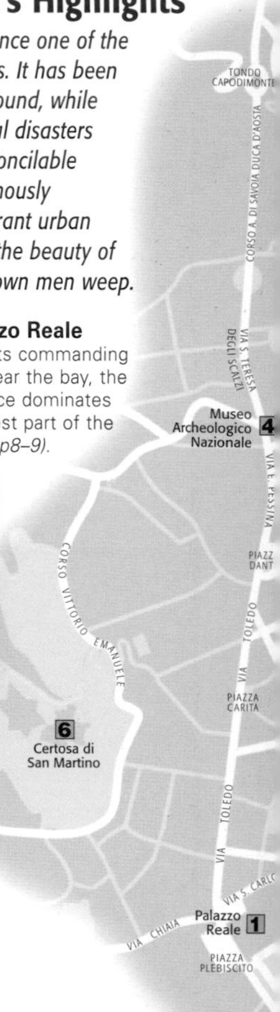

1 Palazzo Reale
With its commanding position near the bay, the Royal Palace dominates the grandest part of the city *(see pp8–9)*.

2 Castel Nuovo
Despite its bulky towers of volcanic stone, this Renaissance castle also features one of the most graceful archway entrances of the period, delicately carved in the purest white marble *(see pp10–11)*.

3 Duomo
In effect, Naples' cathedral is at least three churches in one, including a treasure-laden Palaeo-Christian basilica from the 4th century. The side chapel dedicated to the city's adored patron saint, San Gennaro, is so large and resplendent that it is really a church in its own right *(see pp12–13)*.

4 Museo Archeologico Nazionale
This is the repository of ancient art that has been unearthed from Pompeii and other archaeological digs around Vesuvius. These amazing finds evoke a Classical civilization of great refinement and grandeur *(see pp14–17)*.

5 Capodimonte
What started out as an unassuming hunting lodge soon grew to become a vast royal palace. It is now a museum housing one of Italy's finest collections of art *(see pp18–19)*.

Certosa di San Martino 6

If there is one museum that manages to capture the true Naples, this is it. Come for the unparalleled views from the gardens, for the masterpieces of the Neapolitan Baroque and the world's finest collection of nativity figures *(see pp20–23)*

7 Pompeii & Herculaneum

The world's most famous archaeological site comprises an entire culture caught in a moment of life when Vesuvius erupted nearly 2,000 years ago *(see pp24–7)*.

8 Capri

This small island has had a fabled history of glamour and decadence yet it still remains essentially a simple place *(see pp28–9)*

Ravello 9

High above the gorgeous Amalfi Coast this serenely elegant town offers unforgettable views, gorgeous gardens, aristocratic architecture and poetic inspiration *(see pp30–31)*.

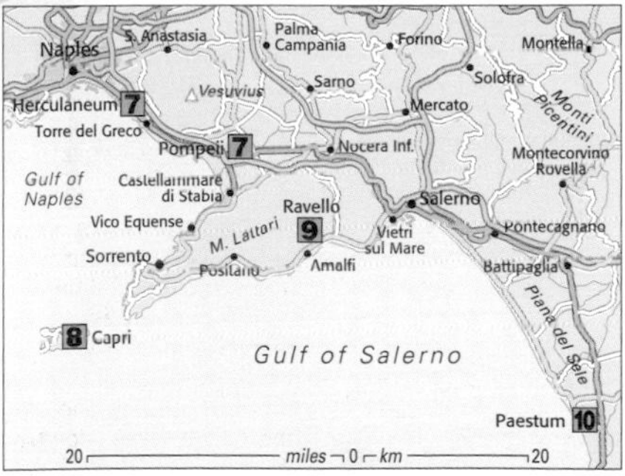

10 Paestum

Some of the best preserved Greek temples in the world stand in timeless splendour on this evocative plain south of Naples *(see pp32–3)*.

TOP 10 Palazzo Reale, Naples

One glance at this imposing Royal Palace and it becomes clear that, in its heyday, Naples was one of Europe's most important cities and home to one of the Mediterranean's most glittering royal courts. Begun in 1600, by order of the Spanish viceroy, it was designed by Domenico Fontana and completed in just two years. However, additions, including the grand staircase, were made over the years, and it was enlarged and redesigned in the 18th and 19th centuries. The edifice was a royal residence until 1946, when the monarchy was exiled for their ill-considered support of Mussolini's Fascist regime.

Palace façade

Caffè Gambrinus ***(see p87)*****, located in the stylish piazza next to the palace, is an excellent and historic choice for a drink, snack or a full meal.**

The ticket office is notoriously hard to find, often confused with the gift shop. It's located to the left of the main entrance, near the corner of the building. It's best to buy an artecard ***(see p122)*** **depending on how many days you plan to be in Naples – it reduces entrance fees to the major sights and you will also often get prioritized entry, saving a great deal of time.**

- *Piazza del Plebiscito*
- *Map N5*
- *081 794 40 21*
- *Open 9am–8pm Mon–Tue, Thu–Sun*
- *Adm €4.00*

Top 10 Features

1. Façade
2. Teatrino di Corte
3. Staircase
4. Decor of the Apartments
5. Furnishings
6. Paintings
7. Sala di Ercole
8. Cappella Palatina
9. Biblioteca Nazionale
10. Gardens & Stables

1 Façade

Dominating the vast Piazza del Plebiscito, the palace's late Renaissance façade of brickwork and grey piperno stone is adorned with giant statues of Naples' foremost kings.

2 Teatrino di Corte

Dating from 1768, this private theatre *(above)* attests to the royal family's passion for comic opera. In the side niches are figures of Apollo and his Muses.

3 Staircase

The monumental staircase *(right)* leads from the central courtyard up to the royal apartments. The original masterpiece dates from 1651; in 1837 it was embellished with marble.

4 Decor of the Apartments

The subject matter of the frescoes *(above)* that decorate the 30 royal apartments was chosen to flatter various royals.

5 Furnishings

Stunning examples of Empire furniture *(right)* predominate in the palace's apartments, much of it of French manufacture. Tapestries adorn many of the rooms, as do exceptional examples of 18th-century marble tables elaborately inlaid with semi-precious stones.

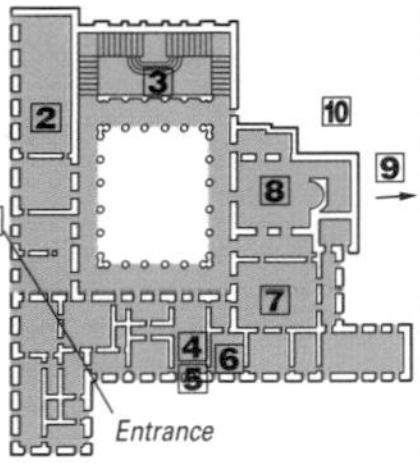

Plan of Palazzo Reale

6 Paintings

Of considerable importance is the abundance of paintings of all genres, including works by Giordano, Guercino, Carracci, Preti *(below)* and Titian. Look, too, for 17th-century Dutch portraits, 19th-century Neapolitan landscape paintings and 18th-century Chinese watercolours.

7 Sala di Ercole

The Hall of Hercules derives its name from the ancient statue displayed here in the 19th century.

8 Cappella Palatina

A 16th-century wooden door, painted in faux bronze, leads to the Royal Chapel, where all the court's religious activities took place. The high altar consists of semiprecious stones set in gilt copper, while the 18th-century nativity scene is a rich study of local life at the time.

9 Biblioteca Nazionale

The massive National Library has at its core the Farnese collection, with books dating from the 5th century. Also here are 1st-century-BC papyri found at Herculaneum.

10 Gardens & Stables

To the north of the palace, the gardens *(above)*, laid out in 1841, afford views of the hill of San Martino in one direction, and of Vesuvius and the bay in the other. The old stables are now used for special exhibitions.

Guide to the Palazzo Reale

You are free to walk around the inner courtyard and the gardens at your leisure, without a ticket, as well as to visit the National Library. To visit the Royal Apartments, buy your ticket and take the grand staircase up to the left only, after which you may visit the rooms in whatever order you wish and stay as long as you like.

The Farnese Hercules statue, once in the Sala di Ercole, can now be seen in the Museo Archeologico **See pp14–17**

TOP 10 Castel Nuovo, Naples

The Castel Nuovo is more commonly known locally as the Maschio Angioino, *a name that clearly dates the fortress's origins to the reign of Charles I of Anjou in the late 13th century. It was officially called the "New Castle" to distinguish it from existing ones, namely the Ovo and the Capuano. During the reign of Robert of Anjou, the place became an important cultural centre, attracting such greats as Petrarch, Boccaccio and Giotto for productive sojourns. It was the Spanish conquerors from Aragon, however, who, in the 15th century, gave it is present-day militaristic look as well as Renaissance embellishments. Currently the castle houses Naples' Civic Museum and administrative offices.*

Bas-relief, Triumphal Arch

A good choice for a meal, inside nearby Galleria Umberto I, is Caffè Roma, where you'll find a tempting array of freshly made local dishes *(see p82).*

If sections of the castle are closed, enquire at the information office located in the courtyard and someone may be kind enough to let you in for a look.

- *Piazza Municipio*
- *Map N5*
- *081 795 20 03*
- *Open Jun–Mar: 9am–7pm Mon–Sat (daily Apr–May)*
- *Adm €5.00*

Top 10 Features

1. Architecture
2. Triumphal Arch
3. Sala dei Baroni
4. Cappella Palatina
5. Museo Civico
6. Paintings of Naples
7. Dungeons
8. Inner Courtyard
9. Excavations
10. Views

1 Architecture

In the 15th century five cylindrical towers were added *(right)*, as was a Catalan courtyard and the Hall of the Barons.

2 Triumphal Arch

Inspired by ancient Roman antecedents, the arch was built in 1443 to celebrate King Alfonso V of Aragon and features sculpted bas-reliefs.

3 Sala dei Baroni

In 1486 Ferrante I of Aragon invited barons who were plotting against him to a ball here, whereupon he had them all executed. Today the hall is notable for its splendid vaults *(above)*.

4 Cappella Palatina

The castle's main chapel is the only remaining part of the original Angevin palace. It houses frescoes from the 14th to 16th centuries, as well as a fine Renaissance sculpted tabernacle *(right)*.

6 Paintings of Naples
The second floor of the museum focuses on Neapolitan works of a secular nature from the 18th to 20th centuries. Delightful sculptures include *scugnizzi* (street urchins), especially the famous *Fisherboy* by Vincenzo Gemito *(left)*.

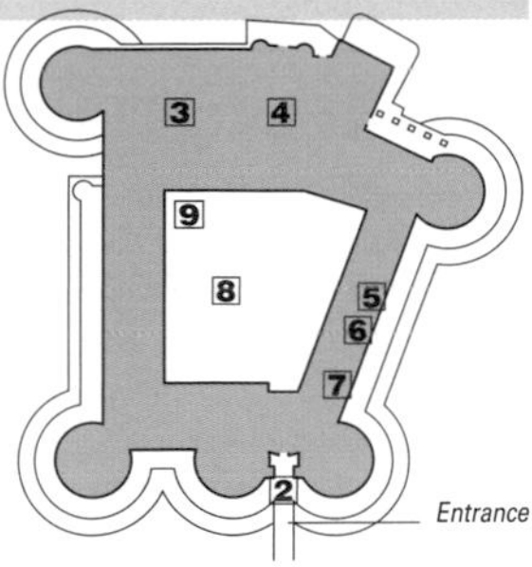

Plan of Castel Nuovo

7 Dungeons
Legend has it that prisoners would regularly disappear from these dungeons without a trace, and the cause was discovered to be a huge crocodile that would grab their legs through a drain hole and drag them away. True or not, the hole now has a grating over it.

8 Inner Courtyard
This harmonious space *(right)* has typically Catalan features, such as the "depressed" arches – broader and flatter than Italian types – and an external grand staircase.

9 Excavations
In the left corner of the courtyard visitors can view archaeological excavations through a glass floor. Macabre surprises include skeletons of monks from an early convent on the site.

10 Views
One of the best aspects of a visit to the castle is taking in the magnificent views from its upper walls and terraces. Panoramas include Mount Vesuvius and, on a clear day, even the Sorrentine Peninsula.

5 Museo Civico
On the first floor of the Civic Museum are paintings and sculptures, including a 16th-century *Adoration of the Magi* in which the Wise Men are portraits of kings Ferrante I and Alfonso II, and Emperor Charles V. Also here are 15th-century bronze doors, depicting royal victories over rebellious barons *(right)*.

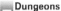

From Fortress to Civic Park
The castle still retains a defensive look – most notably the sloping base surmounted by a rim of castellated battlements – and in the 16th century an enclosing ring wall was added, with bastions of its own, which hid the castle from view and gave the entire area an even more ominous feel. Following Italy's Unification, however, the wall was demolished and the area was laid out with avenues, lawns and flower gardens, lessening the forbidding aspect of the place.

TOP 10 Duomo, Naples

Naples' cathedral originally dates from the 4th century AD with the founding of the Basilica of Santa Restituta, but two centuries later the Basilica del Salvatore was built at right angles to the first and this is the site now occupied by the Duomo. Work on the Duomo as we see it today began in the 13th century during the reign of Charles I of Anjou, but over the centuries it has suffered repeated earthquake damage and has consequently been restored and renovated according to prevailing tastes of the times. The result is an amazingly rich array of art and architecture going back 2,000 years.

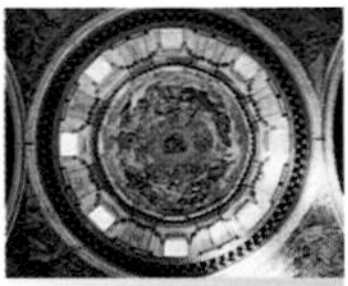

Domed ceiling, Cappella di San Gennaro

For pizza without queues, visit Ristorante-Pizzeria Lombardi *(see p79)*.

You will doubtless encounter large groups being led around by docents. No one will mind if you join the group, at least for a bit; otherwise, take your own personal tour to another part of the cathedral until the crowds move on.

- *Via Duomo 147*
- *Map P1*
- *081 44 90 97*
- *www.duomodinapoli.com*
- *Duomo: Open 8am–12:30pm, 4:30–7pm Mon–Sat; 8am–1:30pm, 5–7:30pm Sun; Free*
- *Archaeological Area and Baptistry: Open 9am–noon, 4:30–6:30pm Mon–Sat, 8:30am–1pm Sun; Adm €3.00*

Top 10 Features

1. Façade & Portals
2. Interior & Ceiling
3. Cappella di San Gennaro
4. Relics
5. Cappella Minutolo
6. Crypt of the Succorpo
7. Font
8. Santa Restituta
9. Baptistry
10. Archaeological Area

1 Façade & Portals

The façade of Naples' cathedral *(below)* is a Neo-Gothic affair restored in the early 20th century but it is graced by three portals that date back to the 1400s.

2 Interior & Ceiling

The interior cathedral never fails to dazzle. The floorplan is 100 m (330 ft) long, with a nave and two aisles lined with chapels *(centre)*. Sixteen pillars support arches flanked by ancient granite columns.

3 Cappella di San Gennaro

Built in the 1600s, this Baroque extravaganza to the centre-right of the nave employed marble and precious metals and the great artists of the day to decorate its walls and ceiling.

The Duomo is dedicated to Our Lady of the Assumption, but it is commonly known as the church of San Gennaro.

4 Relics

The main reliquary is a gold bust of San Gennaro containing his skull bones. The reliquary of his blood *(above)* has ampoules of dried fluid.

8 Santa Restituta

Naples' oldest building was commissioned by Emperor Constantine, who made Christianity the religion of the Roman Empire. Inside are a Romanesque fresco and mosaics dating from 1322.

5 Cappella Minutolo

This chapel is one of the best-preserved examples of the Gothic style of the 13th and 14th centuries. The Cosmatesque mosaic floor and altar frescoes are of particular note.

6 Crypt of the Succorpo

The complexity and originality of this Renaissance chapel have led scholars to attribute the design to Bramante. Adornments include paintings and sculptures by artists such as Pietro Bernini.

7 Font

The cathedral's main baptismal font *(below)* dates from 1618. The basin is made of Egyptian basalt, and there are Greek sculptures and an episcopal throne dating from 1376 in the right-hand nave.

9 Baptistry

This is the oldest baptistry in the western world *(below)*. It was built towards the end of the 4th century and is adorned with splendid mosaics. The font itself is thought to have come from an ancient temple to Dionysus.

10 Archaeological Area

From Santa Restituta, you can enter the archaeological area *(left)*, with remnants of Greek, Roman and early Christian structures, including walls, columns, mosaics, religious buildings and Greek and Roman roads. There is some evidence of *insulae* (apartment blocks) having been here in Roman times.

San Gennaro

Naples' patron saint was an early Christian who battled the disapproval of Emperor Diocletian. Bent on stamping out the off-shoot Jewish sect, the emperor set about slaughtering Christians, but Gennaro survived by his faith until he was finally beheaded in AD 305. His body and vials of blood were preserved in the Catacombs of San Gennaro *(see p54)* until they were moved here. Later, a believer discovered that his dried blood miraculously liquefied on demand, an event that became a city-wide cult.

The bust of San Gennaro is on view only during the thrice-yearly miracle of the liquefaction of his blood (May, Sep and Dec).

TOP 10 Museo Archeologico Nazionale

Among the world's top museums of ancient art, Naples' Archaeological Museum overwhelms with its wealth of beautiful and priceless objects. The building itself was built in the 16th century as headquarters for the royal cavalry and converted a century later into a university. Another century saw it turned into a museum, the Real Museo Borbonico, to house the Farnese collection and the fascinating finds that were brought to light at Pompeii and Herculaneum. Now the Farnese Collection is broken up, with the paintings at Capodimonte and the books in the National Library, leaving this museum to focus on its ancient marvels.

Museum façade

For an array of places to eat and drink, head for Piazza Bellini. Caffè Arabo is a delicious choice *(see p77)* – take a table outside so that you can gaze upon the excavated Greek walls in the centre of the piazza.

Make an appointment to tour Il Gabinetto Segreto at the entrance to the museum. You will be given a time and a choice of languages.

- *Piazza Museo 19*
- *Map N1*
- *081 564 89 41*
- *www.archeona.arti.beniculturali.it*
- *Open 9am–7:30pm Wed–Mon*
- *Adm €6.50*
- *Il Gabinetto Segreto: Open for tours 9:30am–1:30pm, 2:30–6:30pm Wed–Mon*

Top 10 Exhibits

1. Marble Sculpture
2. Bronze Sculpture
3. Friezes, Frescoes & Murals
4. Mosaics
5. Il Gabinetto Segreto
6. Glass & Stone Vessels
7. Pottery & Metal Vessels
8. Incised Gems, Coins & Epigraphs
9. Weapons, Jewellery & Domestic Items
10. Egyptian & Prehistoric Items

1 Marble Sculpture

Some of the world's most renowned ancient Classical sculptures are housed here, by artists such as Phidias, Lysippus, Praxiteles and Polyclitus. Also of great importance are the striking Greek and Roman portrait busts *(above)*. Ground floor.

2 Bronze Sculpture

A true treasure-trove of bronze masterpieces, including a Resting Hermes, Fauns, Water-Bearers and a host of statues and busts *(above)*. First floor.

3 Friezes, Frescoes & Murals

These Roman works excavated from Pompeii *(below)* disclose a great deal about the society and religion of the time. First floor.

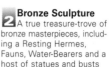

The museum is constantly being reorganized, so be prepared for changes in exhibition spaces and closures of some sections.

4 Mosaics
Romans had a love of mosaic decoration, for both floors and walls. Small chips of coloured glass and stone *(tesserae)* were used to create scenes of every genre. Mezzanine.

5 Il Gabinetto Segreto
Once held too obscene to be shown, this collection can now be seen by appointment. In frescoes, sculptures, mosaics and more, we can sense the exuberant sexuality of the ancient world. Mezzanine.

6 Glass & Stone Vessels
Masters at producing coloured and transparent glassware *(below)*, the Romans carried these techniques to artistic heights. The celebrated Farnese Cup is engraved, in semiprecious stone with layers of sardonyx and agate. First floor.

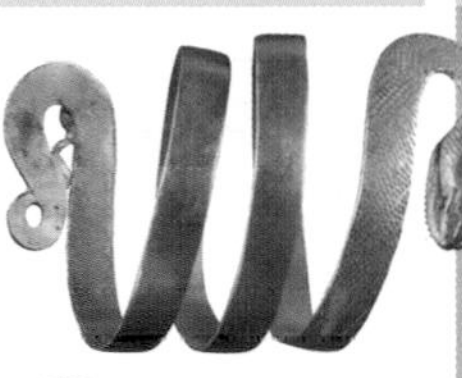

9 Weapons, Jewellery, & Domestic Items
Shields, helmets and swords remind us that the ancient world was one of combat, but metalsmiths also made adornments such as armlets *(above)*. Domestic items include lamps and cups. Basement.

10 Egyptian & Prehistoric Items
This collection contains examples of art from the Ancient Kingdom (2700–2200 BC) down to the Roman age. Funereal steles, vases, statuettes, sarcophagi and mummies can be seen here. Basement & first floor.

7 Pottery & Metal Vessels
Pottery here includes Greek and Etruscan *kraters* and Roman terracotta jars, vases and figurines. Grecian urns, with red figures on black backgrounds *(above)*, depict a variety of scenes. Cups and lanterns also feature. First floor.

8 Incised Gems, Coins & Epigraphs
The collection of incised gems contains Greek and Roman pieces, while bronze, silver and gold coins *(left)* include some from Magna Graecia. Ancient written records include the bronze *Tavole di Eraclea* (3rd century BC). Ground floor.

Building the Collection
The vast Farnese Collection, inherited by King Ferdinando IV from his mother Elisabetta Farnese in the 18th century, forms the core of the museum, including one of the most important and largest assemblages of Roman antiquities in existence. Excavations around Vesuvius *(see pp24–7)* added to the marvellous bounty. In the past 200 years the inventory of world-class treasures has been augmented by numerous important aristocratic collections, including the Bourbon, the Borgia, the Orsini, the Picchianti and the Astarita collections.

Left **Farnese Cup** Centre **Dancing Faun** Right **The Doryphorus**

Top 10 Individual Masterpieces

1 Farnese Bull

Found in the Baths of Caracalla in Rome, this is the largest sculptural group to have survived from antiquity. One of the best-known pieces in the Farnese Collection, it recounts the story of Dirce, who ill-treated Antiope and is being punished by the latter's sons by being tied to a bull. It is probably a copy – though some claim it may be the original – of a 2nd-century BC Greek work and is Hellenistic in its execution. Ground floor.

2 Farnese Hercules

Created and signed by Glykon of Athens, this powerful marble sculpture is a copy and enlargement of a lost bronze original by the 4th-century BC Greek master Lysippus. It was also found in the ruins of the Baths of Caracalla in Rome, where it is thought that it served as magnificent decoration for the imperial pleasure-dome. The work shows the mythical hero at rest, exhausted after having completed his round of 12 superhuman tasks. Ground floor.

Farnese Hercules

3 The Doryphoros

This is the most complete replica of the celebrated bronze original, created in about 440 BC by Polyclitus of Argos. The name means "spear-bearer" and one can see that the figure once held a spear in his left hand. It is thought to represent Achilles, the hero of the Trojan War, and the statue was known in ancient times as the Canon, exhibiting perfect proportions in every aspect of its depiction of the human form. The sculptor developed a complex theory of measurements, related to music, for the ideal construction of the human body. Ground floor.

4 Dancing Faun

A more joyous image of freedom and exuberant health would be hard to imagine. This bronze was found in Pompeii's Casa del Fauno, to which it gives its name, as a decoration in the atrium to greet arriving guests. Two ancient replicas are known of this Hellenistic figure, so it must have been a popular and inspiring object. Mezzanine.

5 Hermes at Rest

Were it not for the wings on his feet, one might suppose that this extremely boyish Hermes (Mercury) was just a young athlete taking a break from his exertions rather than a god. The proportions of this eclectic sculpture were inspired by the work of Lysippus. Mezzanine.

Sleeping and Drunken Satyrs

6 Sleeping and Drunken Satyrs

Satyrs to the ancients were always a symbol of pure hedonism – not just sexual licence, but every form of ease and indulgence. These two figures, from the Villa dei Papiri *(see p26)*, express a light-hearted indolence that is as implicitly erotic as it is earthy. The ancients believed that physical pleasure and delight were part of man's divine essence and gifts from the gods. First floor.

7 Alexander the Great Mosaic

Found as a floor decoration in Pompeii's Casa del Fauno, a grand aristocratic mansion of the 2nd century BC, this Hellenistic mosaic is certainly one of the most elegant and exciting to have survived. The subject is the routing of Darius's Persian armies by Alexander the Great's cavalry. The monumentality of the work is impressive and it is almost certainly a copy of a lost painting of great importance, possibly by Philoxeno. Fragmentary as it is, there are still some one million *tesserae* (tiles) in its composition. Mezzanine.

Achilles and Chiron

8 Achilles and Chiron

Retrieved from the so-called Basilica in Herculaneum, this fresco depicts the young hero of the Trojan War with his mentor, the centaur Chiron. Since this large work was decoration for a public building, the message is clear – heed the elemental forces of Nature (symbolized by the centaur) to find balance and fulfilment in life. The image is based on a famous sculptural group, probably Greek, now lost but known to have stood in ancient Rome, as recorded by Pliny the Elder. First floor.

9 Sacrifice of Iphigenia

Found in Pompeii, in the so-called House of the Tragic Poet, this famous painting shows the dramatic moment when the sacrifice of Iphigenia is halted by the intervention of Artemis (Diana), who kills a deer instead. The fresco was once considered a faithful copy of a painting by the Greek artist Timante, but it is now thought to be an original Roman depiction – due primarily to its overall lack of compositional unity. First floor.

10 Farnese Cup

The star of the museum's cameo and incised gem collection is this glistening masterpiece, carved from a single piece of stone, specifically chosen by the artist for its layering of agate and sardonyx. The outer face of the cup has an image of Medusa; inside is an allegorical scene that probably alludes to the fertility of the Nile. The cup was produced in Egypt in the 2nd or 1st century BC. Ground floor.

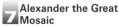

Top 10 Capodimonte, Naples

Construction began on this royal palace, museum and porcelain factory in 1738, under architect Antonio Medrano, and it has been home to a large part of the Farnese Collection since 1759. After the French occupation in 1799 the collection was briefly dispersed, with some pieces taken away to France, but they were later returned following the restoration of the Bourbons in 1815. With the Unification of Italy, in 1860, the palace and its treasures became the property of the House of Savoy and the residence of the Dukes of Aosta until 1947. It was opened to the public in 1957 and restored in 1996, with the Neapolitan and contemporary art galleries added in 1997.

Capodimonte façade

Choose the Museum Café for refreshment – it's located down the arcaded corridor away from the shop in the direction of the toilets and then right; follow the signs.

Public transport in Naples is not for the sensitive or inexperienced; for most, the best way to get up to the museum is to take a taxi. However there are buses from Via Toledo that run up the hill.

- *Porta Grande via Capodimonte, Porta Piccola via Miano 2*
- *Map K1*
- *081 749 91 11*
- *Museum: Open 8:30am–7:30pm Tue–Sun; Adm €7.50*
- *Park: Open 8am–sunset daily; Free*

Top 10 Features

1. Palazzo Reale
2. Pre- and 14th-Century Art
3. 15th-Century Art
4. 16th-Century Art
5. 17th-Century Art
6. 18th-Century Art
7. Porcelain Parlour
8. Drawings & Graphic Works
9. Decorative Arts
10. 19th-Century & Modern Art

1 Palazzo Reale

The palace was first conceived as a hunting lodge by Charles III, but the plans grew into a three-storey structure set in a 7-sq km (2.5-sq mile) park.

2 Pre- and 14th-Century Art

Most of the earliest Italian art in the museum was acquired in the 19th and 20th centuries. Important works include Simone Martini's lavish Gothic masterpiece *San Ludovico di Tolosa (above)*.

3 15th-Century Art

Powerful works here include Botticelli's *Madonna with Child and Angels* and Bellini's sublime *Transfiguration (below)*.

4 16th-Century Art

Here you'll find a serene *Assumption of the Virgin* by Pinturicchio, an *Assumption* by Fra' Bartolomeo and works by Titian and Raphael.

5 17th-Century Art

Strongest of all the works here is Caravaggio's *Flagellation of Christ* and Artemisia Gentileschi's horrifying *Judith and Holofernes (right)*.

6 18th-Century Art

Neapolitan artist Francesco Solimena is well represented here, most especially by his opulent portrait of a courtier, Principe Tarsia Spinelli. Other canvases provide us with period views of Naples *(left)* and its bay and other scenes, including one of Vesuvius in eruption by Pierre-Jacques-Antoine Volaire.

7 Porcelain Parlour

This parlour *(left)* was designed for Queen Maria Amalia. Painted and gilded porcelain assumes the shapes of festoons, musical instruments and figurative scenes.

8 Drawings & Graphic Works

Sketches and studies by some of the greatest artists can be seen here, including works by Fra' Bartolomeo, Raphael and Michelangelo.

9 Decorative Arts

The palace is replete with decorative arts, from ivory carvings to tapestries, to 18th- and 19th-century furniture made for the royal family *(above)*.

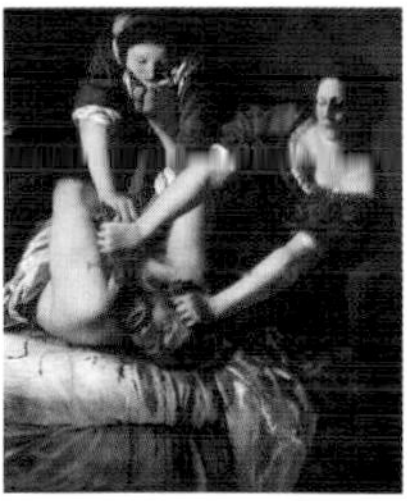

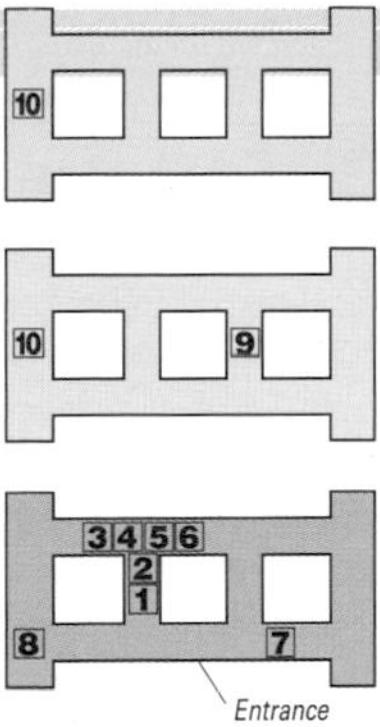

Plan of Capodimonte

Key

- Ground Floor
- First Floor
- Second Floor

10 19th-Century & Modern Art

History paintings and landscapes, by local and visiting artists, dominate this part of the collection. Especially endearing are the sculptures of street urchins by Vincenzo Gomito, but the signature modern work is a complete departure – Andy Warhol's cheerfully garish *Vesuvius*.

Royal Porcelain Factory

Charles of Bourbon established the Reale Fabbrica delle Porcellane in 1739 and it quickly became celebrated for the refinement of its porcelain creations. The factory flourished until 1759, when the king returned to his native Spain and took it and the staff with him, but it reopened in 1771, and production of top-quality pieces recommenced. The mark for objects made here was generally a crowned "N" in blue on the underside.

The Royal Porcelain Factory is today home to the Institute for the Porcelain and Ceramics Industry.

TOP 10 Certosa di San Martino

In 1325 Charles, Duke of Calabria began construction on what is now one of the richest monuments in Naples, the monastery of San Martino. The extensive layout of the place, serenely ensconced just below the massive Castel Sant' Elmo, is nothing less than palatial, boasting two fine cloisters and a dazzling array of architectural and artistic wonders. The Carthusian monks were avid collectors and between the 16th and 18th centuries commissioned the greatest artists of the day to embellish their impressive edifice. Given its commanding position, the finest in Naples, the monastery also enjoys the most spectacular views of the entire city, its bay, the Sorrentine peninsula and Vesuvius.

Chiostro Grande

The best place for a quick and delicious snack is Arx *(Via Tito Angelini 57 • Piazzale San Martino • 081 556 88 58 • €).* They serve wonderful sandwiches, great pizza and creamy desserts with fresh fruit toppings.

Most of the ground floor is accessible, but the upper and lower floors seem to be under permanent restoration. If there is something you particularly want to see, ask one of the custodians and the locked rooms may be opened for you.

- *Largo San Martino 5*
- *Map L4*
- *081 578 17 69/ 558 59 42*
- *Open 8:30am–7:30pm Tue–Sat, 9am–7:30pm Sun*
- *Adm €6.00*

Top 10 Features

1. Façade
2. Church
3. Paintings & Frescoes
4. Sculpture & Marble Decor
5. Choir & Sacristy
6. Chapels & Subsidiary Rooms
7. Chiostro Grande
8. Monks' Cemetery
9. Quarto del Priore
10. Gardens & Belvederes

1 Façade

Although originally Gothic in style, the façade has mostly been overlain with Baroque decoration, including the large round windows.

2 Church

The nave of the church is a riot of Baroque art – the most complete record of Neapolitan art from the 17th and 18th centuries crowded into a single space.

3 Paintings & Frescoes

Dominating the ceiling is the *Ascension of Jesus* by Lanfranco, while the counter-façade has a lovely *Pietà* by Stanzione.

4 Sculpture & Marble Decor

The altar, designed by Solimena, sports silver putti by Giacomo Colombo and silver angels by Sanmartino, who did many of the marble figures *(left)* that adorn the chapels.

5 Choir & Sacristy

The richly carved walnut choir stalls *(above)* were executed between 1629 and 1631 by Orazio de Orio and Giovanni Mazzuoli. Note the cherubs and the abundance of volute curves.

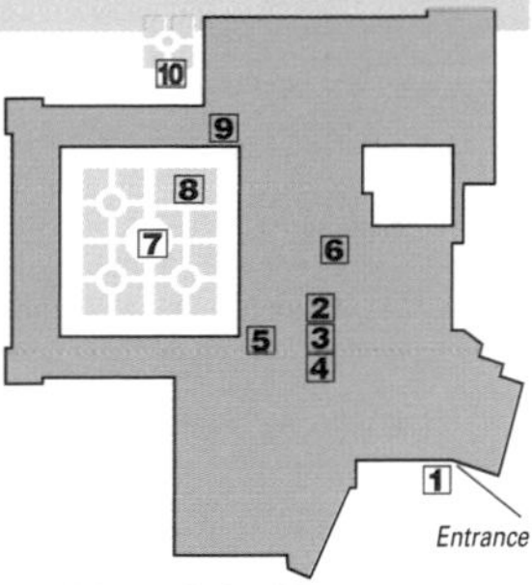

Plan of the Monastery

6 Chapels & Subsidiary Rooms

The eight chapels are decorated in a unified style consistent with the main part of the church. All of them are rich with brightly coloured marbles and opulent gilded stucco trim *(above)*.

7 Chiostro Grande

The Large Cloister *(below)* is one of Italy's finest, with a 64-marble-columned portico designed in the 16th century in Renaissance style.

8 Monks' Cemetery

Taking up a corner of the Chiostro Grande is a plot where a small number of monks have been laid to rest *(below)*.

9 Quarto del Priore

These were the quarters of the monastery's Prior, the only one of the monks who was allowed contact with the outside world. Aristocratic furnishings and priceless works of art adorn the walls.

10 Gardens & Belvederes

One of the most satisfying aspects of the Certosa are its gardens. Not only are the views from here picture-perfect *(above)*, but the gardens themselves are lush and fragrant, with flower and fruit-tree plantings, fountains and marble benches.

The Monastery's Guardian

Before entering the Certosa, be sure to take in the looming castle hovering above it. The monastery was built directly beneath Castel Sant'Elmo for the protection that it afforded. The original structure dates from Angevin times, but it was rebuilt by the Spanish in the 16th century on a six-pointed star design. Its original name was Sant'Erasmo, after the hill it stands on, but the name became corrupted over the centuries, first to Sant'Eramo, then Sant'Ermo, and finally Sant'Elmo.

Left **Monks of Certosa, Micco Spadaro** Right **Tavola Strozzi, Italian Renaissance**

TOP 10 Pinacoteca and Museum Exhibits

1 Early International Renaissance Art

The most outstanding piece here is the triptych by Jean Bourdichon of the Virgin and Child and saints John the Baptist and John the Evangelist (c.1414). The work employs masterful perspective and anatomical detail.

2 Early Italian Renaissance Art

Of special note here is a 15th-century view of Naples, the *Tavola Strozzi*, by an unknown artist and the first painted view of the city from the sea. Sculptures include a marble *Madonna and Child*, attributed to Tino di Camaino.

3 High Renaissance Art

The most significant works here are marble sculptures, including a late 16th-century work by Pietro Bernini, *Madonna with Child and St John the Baptist as a Child*. Its twisting composition, with St John kissing the Child's foot and Mary looking on, embodies tenderness.

Madonna with Child and St John the Baptist as a Child, Pietro Bernini

4 Baroque Art

This era is the collection's strongest suit. Sculptures include a *Veiled Christ* in terracotta by Corradini and a *St Francis* in marble by Sanmartino. A devout Lanfranco painting, *Madonna with Child and Saints Domenico and Gennaro*, is typical of the age.

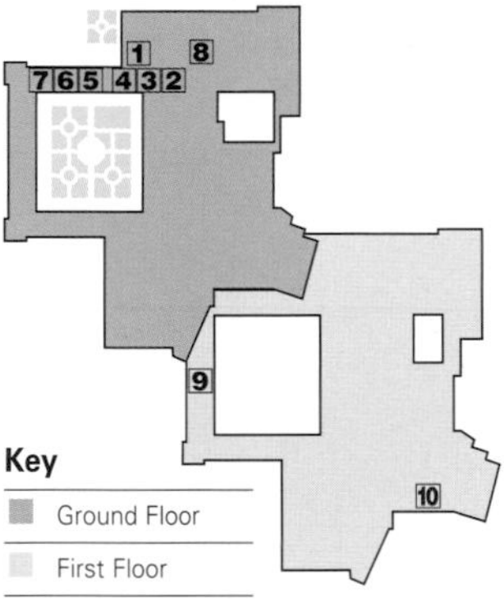

5 Jusepe Ribera

The great Spanish artist, who worked in Naples for most of his life, was appreciated for his dramatic style *(see p45)*. His *St Sebastian* is one of the most powerful works, showing the ecstatic face of the young man, his body pierced with arrows.

6 Micco Spadaro

This artist's *Martyrdom of St Sebastian* provides an interesting contrast with Ribera's work. Rather than focus on the man in close-up, he is shown off to the right being tied up, just before Roman soldiers let their arrows fly. Another Spadaro work shows the monks of the Certosa thanking Christ for sparing them from the plague, with a view of Naples' bay through the arcades.

For opening times to the museum **See p20**

7 Stanzione

Stanzione's *Baptism of Christ* is noteworthy for the luminous way the flesh is rendered, employing pronounced effects of *chiaroscuro* (light and shade).

8 Nativity Collection

Of all the priceless nativity scenes and figures here, the Cuciniello Presepe is by far the most elaborate. Quite lost is the manger scene amid 180 shepherds, 10 horses, 8 dogs, folk going about their business, a Moroccan musical ensemble and much more. Lighting effects create dawn, day, dusk and night.

9 Glass, Porcelain and Gold

The array of objects here goes back to the 1500s and includes painted plates, vases, tiles, pitchers, mirrors and figurines. Subject matter ranges from religious, such as a coral and gold Crucifix, to mythological, to scenes from daily life.

10 Neapolitan 19th-Century Art

Pre- and post-Unification was a time when Italians awoke to their cultural heritage and began to capture it in art. City views and its environs are informative of bygone days, as are the portraits.

Nativity Scenes

The custom of nativity scenes is traditionally traced to December 1223, when St Francis of Assisi celebrated mass before a sculptured group of the Holy Family flanked by a live ox and ass. However, in 1025, there was already a church of Sancta Maria ad Praesepem in Naples, where a representation of the Nativity became the focus of devotion. Called presepio, *derived from the Latin* praesepe *or "feeding trough", referring to the Christ Child's initial resting place, the art of the nativity scene grew to become a major undertaking in the 1600s. Kings and queens would vie with each other to gather together the most impressive, dazzling, poignant and often humorous display, commissioning the best artists and designers of the day. However it was not until the end of the 19th century that these wonderful works were fully recognized as an artistic genre in their own right. The oldest example of a monumental Neapolitan* presepio *comes from the church of San Giovanni a Carbonara; sculpted by Pietro and Giovanni Alemanno in 1478–84, it originally included 41 life-size wooden figures, of which 19 still survive in the church.*

Nativity figure

Nativity Tableau

The traditional nativity scenes celebrate the glories of Christ's birth in a stable, complete with Mary and Joseph, shepherds and the Three Wise Men. However characters from contemporary life are also often included in the setting.

TOP 10 Pompeii

Two thousand years ago, few people knew that Vesuvius was a volcano, although in AD 62, what turned out to be a premonitory tremor caused damage to the ancient seaside resort of Pompeii as well as to other towns in the vicinity. Years later, many residents were still repairing the damage to their homes and public buildings. Then, in August AD 79, came the most devastating eruption (see p27). *Horrible as it was for those who suffered and died, the result for posterity was the preservation of an entire ancient culture, discovered centuries years later like an enormous time capsule.*

Forum

There are on-site cafés at Pompeii and Herculaneum

On weekend mornings at Pompeii extra buildings are open to visitors; request free coupons as you enter one of the gates.

- *Via Villa dei Misteri 2, Pompei*
- *Map E4*
- *081 536 51 54*
- *Open 8:30am–7:30pm daily (until 5pm Nov–Mar)*
- *Adm €8.50*
- *Herculaneum: Corso Resina 6, Ercolano; 081 739 09 63; Open Apr–Oct: 8:30am–7:30pm daily; Nov–Mar: 8:30am–5pm daily; Adm €8.50*
- *Oplontis: Via Sepolcri 1, Torre Annunziata; 081 862 17 55; Open Apr–Oct: 8:30am–7:30pm daily; Nov–Mar: 8:30am–5pm daily; Adm €5.00*
- *Villas Arianna and San Marco: Via Passeggiata Archeologica, Castellammare di Stabia; 081 871 45 41; Open 8:30am–6pm daily; Free*
- *Crater of Vesuvius: Open 9am–2 hrs before sunset daily; Adm €6.00*

Top 10 Sights

1. Forum
2. Theatre
3. House of Menander
4. Amphitheatre
5. Stabian Baths
6. Brothel
7. House of the Golden Cupids
8. House of the Faun
9. House of the Vettii
10. Via dei Sepulcri & Villa dei Misteri

1 Forum

Every Roman city centred civic, commercial, political and religious life around the Forum *(below)*, generally a long rectangular area.

2 Theatre

The large 2nd-century BC theatre was built in accordance with the Greek system, using the slope of the land for the *cavea* (seating area).

3 House of Menander

This grand house includes an atrium, peristyle, and baths. It proved to be a treasure-trove of silver objects, now on display in Naples' Museo Archeologico.

4 Amphitheatre

Far to the east stands Pompeii's amphitheatre – a typically oval shape, though small by Roman standards *(below)*. It was the first such built for gladiatorial combat.

5 Stabian Baths

On the western side of Via Stabiana are the Stabian Baths, the most ancient structure in Pompeii, dating back to the 4th century BC. The stuccoed vaults in the men's changing room have preserved images of nymphs and cupids.

There are two main entrances, one near the train stop at Porta Marina and one at the other end, in the modern town of Pompei.

6 Brothel

The *lupanarium*, one of the town's brothels, has walls decorated with frescoes depicting erotic acts and giving some clue to the proclivities of the prostitutes behind the closed doors.

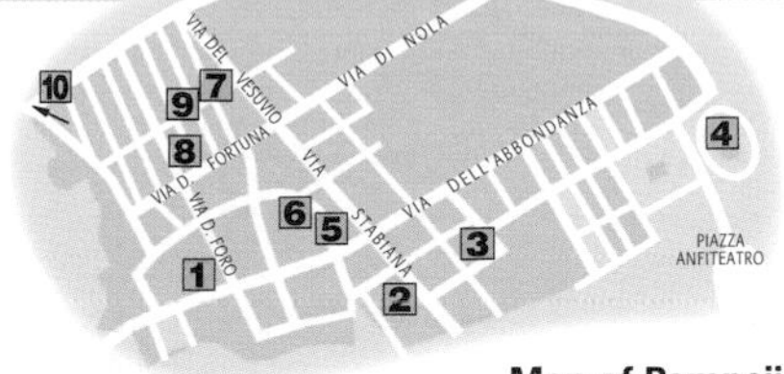

Map of Pompeii

7 House of the Golden Cupids

Named after the gold-leaf decorations of *amorini* (cupids) in the bedroom, this house was owned by the Poppaea family, that of Nero's second wife. The gardens were adorned with sculptures, marble tables and a pool.

9 House of the Vettii

The owners of this house were wealthy merchants. Its interior walls are adorned with splendid paintings and friezes featuring mythological themes *(above)*.

10 Via dei Sepulcri & Villa dei Misteri

The Way of the Tombs lies outside the city gates for fear of the dead bringing bad luck. Beyond this is the 90-room House of the Mysteries *(below)*, where you can peek in to see the marvellous wall paintings.

8 House of the Faun

The 1-m (3-ft) bronze statue of the Dancing Faun *(right)*, found here in the middle of the courtyard pond, accounts for the name of this house, which covered an entire *insula* (city block). Still here are *opus sectile* mosaic marble floors (coloured geometric patterns) as well as wall decorations of merit.

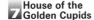

Mount Vesuvius

In ancient times, Vesuvius was simply "the mountain", covered with vegetation and vines, until it famously blew its stack in AD 79. At least five other occurrences have been recorded in the last 400 years and experts estimate that it could erupt again at any time. Its last rumble was in 1944, when the pointed cone disappeared, along with the smoky plume that issued from it.

For more information about visiting Pompeii see p118 and visit the website www.pompeiisites.org

Left **Mosaic, House of Neptune & Amphitrite** Right **Villa of Sabina Poppaea**

TOP 10 Herculaneum, Oplontis & Stabiae

1 Villa dei Papiri

The remains of the resort town of Herculaneum were discovered before Pompeii but were harder to excavate since the city was covered by volcanic mud. Fortunately, this also meant that every aspect was better preserved. This villa was one of the first to be explored, housing art treasures now in the Museo Archeologico *(see pp14–17)*. The papyrus scrolls that give it its name are in the National Library.

2 House of the Stags

The name derives from the sculptured group of stags being attacked by dogs that was found here. Other sculptures include a Satyr with Wineskin and a Drunken Hercules.

3 House of the Mosaic Atrium

This house takes its name from its mosaic floor of black-and-white geometric patterns. Gardens and rooms with views of the sea must have made it a lovely place to relax.

House of the Mosaic Atrium floor

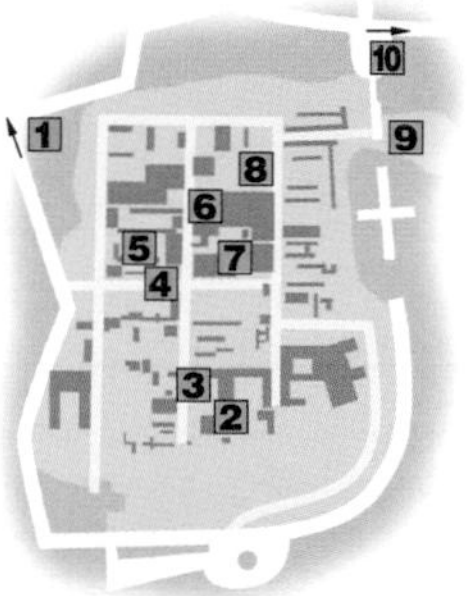

Map of Herculaneum

4 Trellis House

This building provides a wonderfully preserved example of what an ordinary multi-family dwelling was like. Two storeys high, it has a balcony that over-hangs the pavement and its walls are composed of wood and reed laths with crude tufa and lime masonry to fill in the frame.

5 City Baths

Built in 10 BC, these traditional baths are divided into male and female sections, both decorated with the same sea-themed mosaics featuring tritons and fish. At the centre of the complex is an open porticoed area used as a gymnasium.

6 House of Neptune and Amphitrite

This is named after the mosaic of the sea god and his nymph-bride that adorns the fountain in the summer dining room at the back of the house. Other fine mosaics can be seen here too.

For directions and opening times to these sights **See p24**

Trellis House

7 House of the Wooden Partition

A kind of "accordion" partition here was devised to separate the atrium from the *tablinium*, the room of business affairs.

8 Thermopolia

An example of a fast-food outlet of the day. The terracotta amphorae set into the marble counter top would have contained various comestibles. Only wealthy people had facilities to cook food, so most would stop by such a place to eat.

9 Villa of Sabina Poppaea & Villa of Crassus

These aristocratic villas are located in what was once the ancient resort of Oplontis. The complex includes gardens, porticoes, private baths, a pool and astounding wall decorations.

10 Stabian Villas

Set on the Varano Hill, both villas preserve mosaic floors, gardens, peristyles and frescoes. Villa Arianna is named after a fresco of Ariadne being abandoned by Theseus. Villa San Marco sports a gymnasium, pool and interesting frescoes.

The Eruption of AD 79

Pliny the Younger

On 24 August AD 79, Mount Vesuvius suddenly erupted. The apex of the calamity started at about 10am and by 1pm it was all over – all the cities on the mountain's slopes were covered with lava and mud, and Pompeii and its citizens were entirely buried. It lay undiscovered until 1750. Here are the words of Pliny the Younger, who survived to write an eyewitness account of the catastrophic events: "On Mount Vesuvius broad sheets of fire and leaping flames blazed at several points, their bright glare emphasized by the darkness... an ominous thick smoke, spreading over the earth like a flood, enveloping the earth in night... earth-shocks so violent it seemed the world was being turned upside down... the shrill cries of women, the wailing of children, the shouting of men... Many lifted up their hands to the gods, but a great number believed there were no gods, and that this was to be the world's last, eternal night... The flames and smell of sulphur... heralded the approaching fire ...The dense fumes... choked... nearly everyone, to death."

Replica ash figure buried in Pompeii

TOP 10 Capri

Ever since ancient times, this luxuriant, saddle-shaped rock in the Bay of Naples has captured the world's imagination as a place where dreams can be realized and life can become an earthly paradise. Hopes and wishes notwithstanding, the island does have something special, perhaps generated by its sheer dramatic beauty, its crystal-clear waters and its lush vineyards and lemon and olive groves that seem to cover every available corner. The mythic power of Capri runs far deeper and warrants more exploration than the quick package-tour tone it sometimes strikes.

I Faraglioni

In Capri town Da Gemma ***(see p105)*** **provides wonderful views as you dine on pizza, selections from the buffet table, or traditional dishes.**

To get a feel for what the island is all about, take one of the recommended hikes – or better yet, rent a kayak and go exploring along the otherwise inaccessible coastline areas.

- *Map C5, S1*
- *www.caprinet.it*
- *Ferries* (traghetti) *and hydrofoils* (aliscafi) *leave from many ports, including Mergellina and Beverello in Naples, Sorrento, Amalfi, Salerno, Ischia and Castellammare di Stabia. Journey times to Capri are: 80 minutes from Naples; 40 minutes from Sorrento. Hydrofoils take half these journey times.*

Top 10 Sights

1. Marina Grande
2. Capri Town
3. Villa Jovis
4. Arco Naturale
5. Via Krupp & I Faraglioni
6. Marina Piccola
7. Monte Solara
8. Anacapri & Punta Carena
9. Blue Grotto
10. Villa San Michele

1 Marina Grande

Whether by ferry, hydrofoil or private yacht, virtually all visitors to the island arrive at this little port town *(below)*. It's a colourful place, but the bustle is only skin-deep – in reality it's just as laid back as the rest of Capri.

2 Capri Town

Piazza Umberto I, known simply as "Piazzetta" *(centre)* is the town's outdoor salon, filled to the brim with chic bars and restaurants. Night-time is when the true Capri denizens come out to play.

3 Villa Jovis

Emperor Tiberius's 1st-century-AD villa is now in ruins *(above)* but the views of the Bay of Naples, from the highest point at this end of the island, are dazzling.

4 Arco Naturale

Follow signs from the centre of Capri Town for this easy-going walking trail, where a series of rocky staircases offer fine panoramas of the mainland coastline. The imposing Natural Arch itself consists of a huge limestone crag, jutting out and with the bright turquoise sea seen far below.

For more details on ferry services to Capri visit www.caremar.it

5 Via Krupp & I Faraglioni

Via Krupp *(above)* is a switchback path carved into the cliff face. From here there are views of I Faraglioni, rocks isolated out to sea.

6 Marina Piccola

This small harbour has private bathing huts, a pebbly arc of beach, wonderful rocks for diving from and several good fish restaurants.

9 Blue Grotto

The island's most famous attraction is this stunning sea-grotto, of a colour and intensity of blue that can be experienced in no other way *(left)*. Local oarsmen ferry visitors inside.

10 Villa San Michele

Built by a Swedish doctor on the site of one of Tiberius's houses, this villa *(below)* is an eclectic mix of Romanesque, Renaissance and Moorish styles, surrounded by gorgeous gardens.

7 Monte Solaro

No trip to the island is complete without a funicular ride up to Capri's highest peak, from which you can look down on the pastoral timelessness of lemon groves, little white houses, and endless flower gardens that cover the island. Once up top, the 360-degree views are breathtaking.

8 Anacapri & Punta Carena

Before 1877, when the road was built, Anacapri was truly isolated and is still less pretentious than the rest of the island. From here, another great jaunt is to the lighthouse at Punta Carena, where an uncrowded rocky beach awaits, as well as good facilities and excellent restaurants.

A Glamorous Past

Capri emerged on the up-market tourist map in the 19th century, but the high point of famed "Gay Capri" was the early 20th century, when it attracted literati such as Norman Douglas, Graham Greene, Somerset Maugham and Maxim Gorky. More recently, the 1960s, the era known as "Capri People" brought the international jet-set to the island, including *La Dolce Vita* swingers, Hollywood film stars, and even the beautiful newly-wed Jacqueline Kennedy Onassis.

Via Krupp is officially closed, due to the danger of falling rocks, but you may still see locals using it.

Top 10 Ravello

The magnetic beauty of Ravello probably has to do with its many exhilarating contrasts, both visual and cultural. Built boldly upon a rocky spur, separating the Valle del Dragone from the Valle di Maiori, this remarkable city is suspended 350 m (1,150 ft) directly above the azure and turquoise sea of the Gulf of Salerno. From here you can take in the entire Amalfi Coast and its famously picturesque towns in one sweeping glance – and remain transfixed indefinitely by the thoughts of infinity such an awesome view conjures up. A wide range of poetic and artistic souls have taken one look at the place and decided to stay, among them Boccaccio, Wagner, Grieg, Greta Garbo, Leopold Stokowski and, most recently, Gore Vidal.

Scala

Ravello requires a lot of steep walking so bring walking shoes and a maximum dose of energy. The entire town is likely to be a challenge for disabled visitors.

- *Map E4*
- *Villa Cimbrone: Via Santa Chiara 26; 089 85 74 59; Open 9am–30 min before sunset daily; Adm €4.50*
- *Villa Rufolo: Piazza del Duomo; 089 85 70 96; Open 9am–30 min before sunset daily; Adm €4.00*
- *Duomo: Piazza del Duomo; 089 85 83 11; Church: Open 8:30am–1pm, 3–8pm daily; Free; Museum: Open 9:30am–1pm, 3–7pm daily (Nov–Mar Sat–Sun only); Adm €1.50*
- *San Giovanni al Toro: No regular hours; Free*
- *Santa Maria a Gradillo: Open 9am–1pm, 3–6pm daily; Free*
- *Duomo di Scala: Open 8am–noon, 5–7pm daily; Free*

Top 10 Sights

1. Villa Cimbrone
2. Chiostro de San Francesco
3. Villa Rufolo
4. Duomo di Ravello
5. Museo del Duomo
6. Santa Maria a Gradillo
7. San Giovanni al Toro
8. Scala
9. Duomo di Scala
10. Minuta

1 Villa Cimbrone

The creation of an English lord, Ernest Beckett, the house imitates the Moorish style that predominates in Ravello, while its gardens are set about with Classical temples *(below)*.

2 Chiostro de San Francesco

This cloister dates from 1222, when it was jewel of Gothic art. The space was altered in the 18th century but it still retains ancient columns.

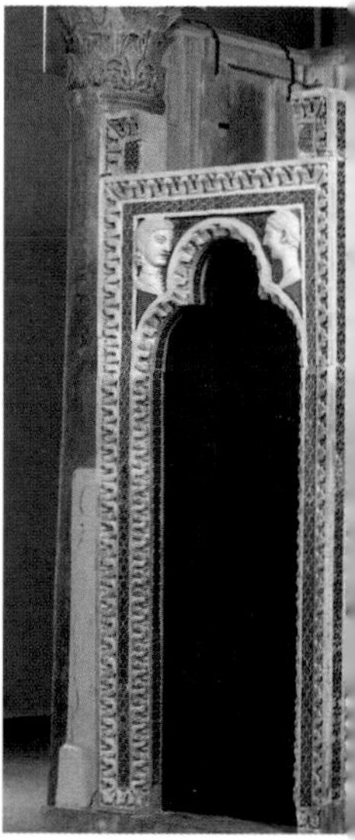

3 Villa Rufolo

The 800-year-old Arab-style palace and its terraced gardens *(below)* have inspired many visitors. The terrace is used in summer for staging concerts.

4 Duomo di Ravello

The 11th-century cathedral is a treasure-trove of works. Its beautiful pulpit (1272) has twisted columns resting on sculpted lions at the base *(centre)*.

5 Museo del Duomo

In the crypt is a collection of Roman and medieval artifacts. Other treasures include a 14th-century marble sarcophagus.

7 San Giovanni al Toro

This church has a mosaic pulpit *(above)* adorned with birds and saints, and supported by Corinthian columns.

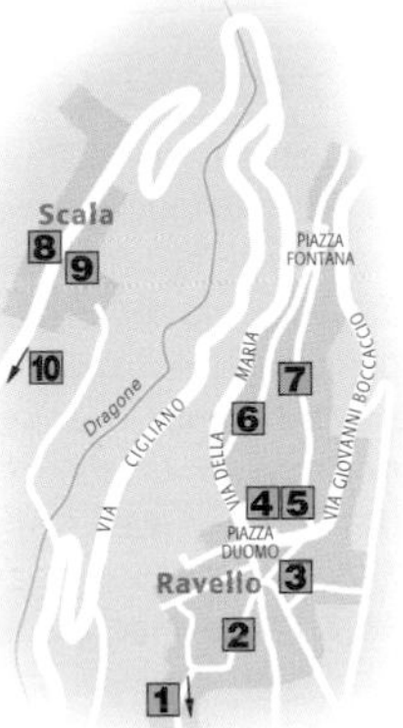

Map of Ravello

10 Minuta

Even higher than Scala, Minuta *(below)* has a pretty 12th-century church with 10 ancient granite columns in the nave and some fine frescoes in the crypt.

Ravello Music Festival

The musical offerings here consist mainly of chamber music, but may include specialist musical events, large and small, and even ballet, all featuring world-class international performers. The festival's beginnings go back to Richard Wagner and Edvard Grieg, the 19th-century composers who found some of their greatest inspiration in these balmy southern climes. For the most part, the concerts take place at Villa Rufolo, but the festival has recently expanded *(see p65)*.

6 Santa Maria a Gradillo

This Romanesque church *(above)* has a belltower in Arab-Sicilian style – in the 12th century Sicily and the Middle East were trading partners with Ravello.

8 Scala

This tiny hamlet, built on a succession of terraces, is worth a visit for the views it affords when you look back at its larger neighbour, Ravello.

9 Duomo di Scala

Scala's cathedral dates from the 13th century. Despite Baroque restructuring, the original wooden crucifix over the main altar and the tomb of the Coppola family have been preserved.

Ravello Music Festival runs from March to November. For details visit the website www.ravelloarts.org

TOP 10 Paestum

Paestum enjoyed 1,000 years of prosperity, first as Greek Poseidonia, founded in the 7th century BC, then under the Lucanians, then the Romans. But the crumbling of the Roman Empire led to the gradual abandonment of the city and with that, the degradation of the fields, which turned into malaria-ridden swamps. No one dared come near the spot until the 18th century when Charles III was having a road built; trees were cut down, and there they were – three intact Greek temples. Much more was discovered in the 20th century.

Amphitheatre

There are plenty of quick snacks and light meals available up and down the tourist strip.

To see the temples at their most evocative, try to visit at dawn or at dusk.

- *Map H6*
- *Site: Open 9am–1 hr before sunset daily*
- *Museum: Open 8:45am–7pm daily (closed 1st & 3rd Mon of each month)*
- *Adm: €4.00 for site or museum, €6.50 for both*

Top 10 Sights

1. Walls
2. Basilica
3. Temple of "Neptune"
4. Amphitheatre
5. Temple of "Ceres"
6. Museum
7. Tomb Frescoes
8. Sculpture
9. Pottery
10. Artifacts

1 Walls
At its peak, the city was large and prosperous, as evidenced by its impressive 5 km (3 miles) of walls, set off with towers and gates at strategic points.

2 Basilica
The oldest temple on the grounds *(above)*, c.530 BC, was most likely dedicated to two deities, Hera and Zeus.

3 Temple of "Neptune"
The last of the three temples to be built, in about 450 BC, is also the finest *(right)*. It may have been dedicated to Neptune (Poseidon), but some scholars argue for Apollo, others for Zeus.

4 Amphitheatre
This Roman structure, dating from the 1st century BC or later, is only partially excavated, the rest lying under the 18th-century road, but some of the exposed part has been rebuilt. Its capacity was small – only about 2,000 – compared to others in the region.

5 Temple of "Ceres"
Votive offerings found here suggest that this small temple *(above)*, further north than the other sites, was actually dedicated to Athena.

6 Museum

Finds from this excavation and several important ones nearby are exhibited here. One of those sites is the Sanctuary of Hera Argiva, built by the Greeks at the mouth of the River Sele in about 600 BC. There is also a collection of Roman finds upstairs.

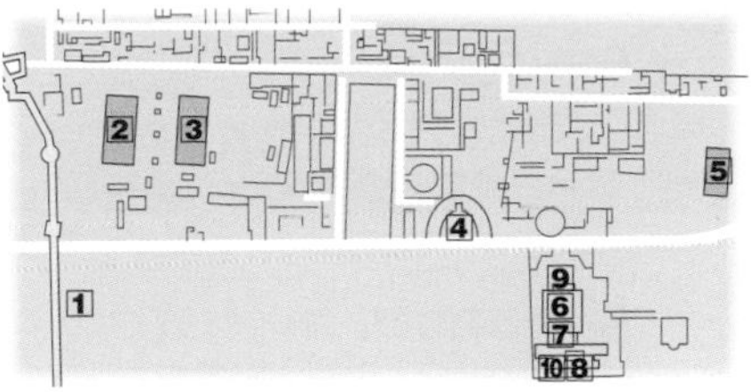

Map of Paestum

7 Tomb Frescoes

Most famous of the exhibits in the museum are the tomb frescoes *(below)*, discovered in 1968 about 1 km (0.5 mile) from Paestum. Virtually the only examples of ancient Greek painting to survive, they are full of light and bright colours. Themes include a banquet of male lovers.

8 Sculpture

Prime examples in this category of the museum include archaic metopes (decorative architectural elements) and one of two dancing girls from the Sanctuary of Hera Argiva *(right)*. They are so well carved in bas-relief that each of the figures seems to be moving independently in space.

9 Pottery

Fine examples of Grecian urns are on view in the museum. These include a krater with red-figured painting on black, depicting a young satyr and a girl reluctant to succumb to his blandishments *(above)*, and an amphora with black figures on red celebrating the fruit of the vine.

10 Artifacts

Other artifacts in the museum include a bronze vase that contained honey, amazingly still liquid at the time it was discovered due to unique atmospheric conditions below ground.

Magna Graecia

Being great seafarers, the ancient Greeks were indefatigable colonizers. Each important city-state sent out expeditions all over the Mediterranean to set up new cities. Magna Graecia (Greater Greece) formed the southern part of the Italian peninsula, along with Sicily, which the Greeks dominated for centuries, until the Romans expanded their hegemony. Paestum (Poseidonia) was one such Greek city, as were Naples (Neopolis), Cumae, and many more.

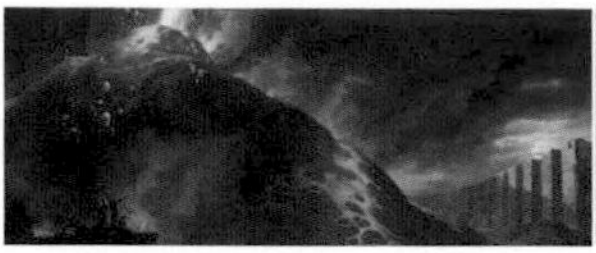

Left **Vesuvius erupts** Right **Garibaldi enters Naples**

Top 10 Moments in History

1 Greek Colonization

From the 8th to the 5th centuries BC this area became an important part of Magna Graecia when Greek city-states set up trading posts here *(see p33)*. In 470 BC Neapolis (New City) was founded, which became modern Naples.

2 Vesuvius Erupts

Around 326 BC the area was absorbed into the Roman Empire and by the 1st century AD Naples was a renowned centre of learning. But in August AD 79 all that changed when Mount Vesuvius suddenly erupted after centuries of dormancy. Within a few hours, entire cities were gone, covered by ash or boiling volcanic mud *(see pp24–7)*.

3 Byzantine Siege

With the fall of the Roman Empire in the 5th century, the area was overrun by tribes from the north, particularly the Goths. In 553 the Byzantine emperor Justinian's chief general Belisarius conquered the zone.

4 Norman Conquest

In 1140 the Norman king Roger II made his triumphant entry into Naples – the Normans had already gained possession of Sicily and most of southern Italy. The once proudly autonomous city now had to take a back seat to Palermo – although wellbeing continued to rise, thanks to the Normans' stability and efficiency.

5 Angevin Capital

In the mid-13th century, the French Anjou dynasty, having taken over the Kingdom of Sicily, shifted its capital to Naples, to the great joy of the residents. Many new buildings were constructed, including, in 1279, the Castel Nuovo *(see pp10–11)*.

6 Sicilian Vespers

With the removal of the capital to the mainland, Sicilian resentment came to a head on Easter Monday 1282. A riot, known as the Sicilian Vespers, left 2,000 Frenchmen dead and initiated a 20-year war. Finally, Sicily was lost and the Angevin kings focused their entire attention on Naples, leading to a period of ever greater prosperity.

Norman king, Roger II

Giving thanks for the end of the plague

7 Plague of 1656

At the beginning of the 17th century Naples was Europe's largest city, with a population of some 300,000, but in 1656 a plague struck. After six months, three-quarters of the population were buried in mass graves.

8 King Charles III Enters in Triumph

In 1734 the Spanish king arrived in Naples. He was heir to the Farnese clan, who were Italian by birth, and transformed his new home town into a city of the Enlightenment.

9 Naples Joins Unified Italy

On 21 October 1860 Naples voted to join a united Italy, under the rulership of an Italian king, Vittorio Emanuele II – Garibaldi had entered the city two months previously to gather up support.

10 Le quattro giornate napoletane

On 27–30 September 1943 Neapolitans showed their true character. After the occupying Nazis threatened to deport all the city's young males, four days of rioting by the populace kept the Germans so busy that the Allies were able to get a toehold and rout the enemy.

Top 10 Historic Figures

1 Parthenope

The siren spurned by Ulysses gave her name to the first Greek colony, in 680 BC, now Pizzofalcone *(see p37)*.

2 Spartacus

This runaway slave led a revolt of the oppressed from headquarters on Vesuvius.

3 Romulus Augustulus

The last emperor of the Western Empire died in Naples in AD 476.

4 Belisarius

The general was sent by the Byzantine Emperor to reconquer much of the Italian peninsula in the 5th century.

5 Pope Innocent II

When the Normans were making progress towards Naples in 1137 the city turned to the pope for help, but the Normans took him prisoner.

6 Queen Joan I

Joan (1343–81) was so loved by the people that they forgave her for plotting the murder of her husband.

7 Tommaso Aniello

This fisherman led a revolt in 1647 against the taxation policies of the Spanish rulers.

8 Maria Carolina of Austria

The sister of Marie Antoinette was the power behind the throne of her husband, Ferdinand IV (1768–1811).

9 King Joachim Murat

Napoleon's brother-in-law ascended the throne of Naples in 1808 but was executed in 1815.

10 Antonio Bassolino

Naples' left-wing mayor from 1993 to 2001 brought about a long-overdue clean up of the city *(see p37)*.

Left **Normans building Castel Nuovo** Right **World War II troops in Naples**

Top 10 Epochs and Eras

1 Ancient Naples

The Greeks may have founded a colony here as early as the 10th century BC. Greek customs and language generally survived during the Roman period, when this was a favourite place for the élite to build holiday villas and to send their young for higher education.

2 The Duchy of Naples

Campania suffered a chaotic period between the 5th and 6th centuries, caused by barbarian invasions, the Gothic war and the Longobard conquest. However, with the reconquest of the coastal areas by the Byzantines, Naples, Sorrento, Amalfi, Salerno and other cities were set up as dukedoms and flourished until the 11th century.

3 Feudal Naples

Naples finally fell to the Normans in 1139. As a result, the established trade with the East went into decline and Naples became a feudal possession, beholden to Sicily. Nevertheless, the Norman period was one of relative prosperity.

4 Growth of the City

With the advent of the Angevins (1266–1442) and the Aragons (1442–1503), Naples was now a modern capital and a powerful employment magnet. This led to severe overcrowding – a chronic Neapolitan problem to this day.

Emperor Charles V of Spain

5 The Viceroys

One of the most significant periods of the two centuries of Spanish viceroys occurred under Emperor Charles V (1516–56), who sent Pedro de Toledo to govern Naples for more than 20 years. The infrastructure, both materially and politically, was strengthened and embellished.

6 Bourbon Naples

In 1734, the kingdom of Naples as an autonomous entity was re-established and Charles of Bourbon was chosen to rule. He ordered notable public works, and presided over the age when Naples was high on the list for Grand Tour enthusiasts.

7 Cholera Epidemic

Although embraced by royalist Neapolitans, Unification resulted in the city's marginalization when Rome was chosen as capital. Not long after, a cholera epidemic in 1884 also made it plain that Naples had problems. The Urban Renewal Plan remedied the overcrowding and poor sewage system to some extent.

8 World War II

Ironically, the gutting of the city's derelict structures was accomplished in large part by World War II bombs, but the city was left devastated and starving. More than 20,000 civilians lost their lives in Allied air raids.

9 Postwar Naples

After the war, ugly apartment blocks throughout the region paved over what had been one of the most beautiful landscapes in the world. Corruption was rife, and *La Camorra* (the local Mafia) gained unprecedented power. In 1980 an earthquake destroyed thousands of shoddy buildings.

10 The New Naples

In 1992 the *Mani pulite* ("clean hands") movement transformed Italian politics and a new generation of leaders came to the fore. Naples' mayor Antonio Bassolino, elected in 1993, began restoration projects, new parks and better public transport that have changed the face of the city.

Scaffolding after the 1980 earthquake

Top 10 Ancient Sites

1 Pompeii & Herculaneum

Frozen in time by a volcanic eruption, these sites provide a view of the world as it was 2,000 years ago *(see pp24–7)*.

2 Capri

Remains of imperial villas that once enjoyed vantage points atop the cliffs can be seen here *(see pp28–9)*.

3 Paestum

Three intact Greek temples standing on a tranquil plain are one of the chief pleasures of the area *(see pp32–3)*.

4 Piazza Bellini

Sections of 5th-century BC Greek walls are found on this square *(see p70)*.

5 Largo Corpo di Napoli

The ancient statue of the Nile on this square was once thought to be that of a woman suckling her young. *Map P3*

6 San Lorenzo Maggiore

Under the church, excavations have revealed 2,000-year-old streets, complete with shops and a porticoed arcade *(see p74)*.

7 Via Anticaglia

Here you can see the remains of brick arches dating from Roman times. *Map P2*

8 Pizzofalcone

Probably founded in the 7th century BC, this was the first settlement in Naples. *Map M6*

9 Phlegraean Fields

Underground cities, craters and mythic ruins all attest to the area's rich archaeological heritage. *Map D3*

10 Cumae

This Greek settlement dates from the 8th century BC and flourished into Roman times *(see p111)*.

Left **Capodimonte artwork** Right **Paestum tomb painting**

TOP 10 Museums and Galleries

1 Museo Archeologico, Naples

An insurpassable museum for the range and beauty of its Greco-Roman art, with important pieces unearthed in Rome and in towns around Vesuvius. The experience is a total immersion in the life of the ancients – their religious beliefs, sports, eating habits, and even their erotic peccadilloes *(see pp14–17)*.

2 Capodimonte, Naples

This world-class museum also owes its main masterpieces to the Farnese Collection. Paintings run the gamut from medieval to contemporary; the porcelain collection also shouldn't be missed *(see pp18–19)*.

3 Museo di San Martino, Naples

This monastery complex is home to several collections of art. The Pinacoteca, comprising part of the Prior's Quarters, is notable for its works from the Renaissance and Baroque eras, many having been commissioned for the monastery. On the upper floors, 19th-century works convey the look and feel of Naples in the days of Italian Unification. A section devoted to Nativity scenes demonstrates the power and beauty of this uniquely Neapolitan art form *(see pp20–23)*.

4 Pinacoteca Girolamini, Naples

For lovers of Neapolitan Baroque this little-known gallery is a must. Part of a monastic complex, there are fine works by Carracciolo, Vaccaro, Giordano, and several by Ribera, featuring his signature taste for the outrageous and extreme.

Via Duomo 142 • Map P2 • Open 9:30am–12:50pm Mon–Fri • Free

5 Museo Civico Filangieri, Naples

The palace itself is an unusual example in Naples of the 15th-century Tuscan Renaissance style, and was donated to the city as a museum in the 19th century. Until 1943 it housed Prince Filangieri's private collection of armour, majolica, coins, porcelain, Nativity figures, sculpture and paintings. Sadly, most of the original pieces were destroyed in World War II, but since then the exhibits have

Statue, Museo Archeologico, Naples

been restored and augmented. They include works by Luini and Ribera. *Via Duomo 288A • Map P2 • Open 9am–7pm Mon–Sat; 9am–1pm Sun • Adm*

6 Museo Nazionale della Ceramica Duca di Martina, Naples

Naples is famous for fine ceramic production and this museum provides rich amplification of the theme. Not only are exquisite Italian pieces found here, by Capodimonte and Ginori artisans, but also splendid creations by the factories of Meissen, Limoges, Sèvres and Saint-Cloud. Majolica works, from medieval times onwards, are also well represented, and the collection of Chinese and Japanese ceramics, from as far back as the T'ang Dynasty, is one of the country's best. *Via Cimarosa 77 • Map J5 • Open for guided tours: 9:30am, 11am, 12:30pm Tue–Sun • Adm*

7 Museobottega della Tarsialignea, Sorrento

Sorrento has been known since the mid-18th century for its fine inlaid wood furniture and objects *(intarsio)* and this museum is devoted to the delicate art. Displayed in a beautifully restored palace, the exhibits also include paintings, old photos and other Sorrentine memorabilia. *Via S Nicola 28 • Map D5 • Open Apr–Oct: 9:30am–1pm, 4–8pm Tue–Sun; Nov–Mar: 9:30am–1pm, 3–7pm Tue–Sun • Adm*

8 Museo Archeologico di Pithecusae, Ischia

Housed in the 18th-century Villa Arbusto, exhibits here illustrate the history of ancient Ischia, from prehistoric to Roman times. Many of the most important objects date back to the 8th century BC, when Ischia was settled by Greeks from the island of Euboea. The most famous pots were found at a nearby necropolis; among these are a typical late geometric *krater*, decorated with a shipwreck scene. *Corso Angelo Rizzoli 210, Lacco Ameno • Map A4 • Open 9:30am–12:30pm, 3–7pm Tue–Sun • Adm*

Machinery, Museo della Carta

9 Museo della Carta, Amalfi

This fascinating museum, set in an old warehouse, preserves one of Europe's first papermaking factories. Visitors can see the original stone vats and machinery downstairs, and there's also an interesting exhibit tracing the history and technical progress of the paper industry over the centuries. *Palazzo Pagliara, Via delle Cartiere 24, Valle dei Mulini • Map E5 • Open 10am–6pm daily • Adm*

10 Museo Archeologico, Paestum

Among this museum's beautiful treasures are ancient Greek tomb paintings that were only discovered on the site in 1968. Other finds include bronze vases, terracotta votive figures and various funerary furnishings *(see pp32–3)*.

Left **Certosa di San Martino** Right **Santa Chiara**

TOP 10 Churches in Naples

1 Duomo

The oldest wing of Naples' cathedral is the city's most ancient surviving building, a Paleo-Christian church dating from the 4th century. The cathedral also has the oldest baptistry in the western world. Archaeological excavations here have revealed structures reaching as far back as the ancient Greeks *(see pp12–13)*.

2 Certosa di San Martino

This sparkling white monastery complex commands the most perfect location in the entire city, attesting to the wealth and power the monks once enjoyed. In the 17th and 18th centuries they commissioned the greatest artists of the day to embellish their church and chambers in Baroque style – the church, in particular, is a flamboyant catalogue of colour and pattern, sporting at least one work by each and every famous hand of the age *(see pp20–23)*.

San Francesco di Paola

3 Santa Chiara

The original church here was built in 1310 and, after various renovations, has been returned to its Gothic style. The most famous feature is the adjoining convent's 18th-century majolica cloister celebrating secular themes *(see p69)*.

4 San Francesco di Paola

A rarity in Naples, this Neo-Classical structure imitates the Pantheon, Rome's great pagan temple to the gods built in the 2nd century AD. Inside and out the basilica is austere, with the exception of the polychrome marble Baroque altar *(see p81)*.

5 Monte di Pietà

This majestic building and its adjoining church were built in the late 1500s as a charitable institute set up to grant loans to the needy. In return, the noblemen who provided this service were guaranteed eternal salvation. Decorated mostly in late-Renaissance style, inside are sculptures by Pietro Bernini and frescoes by Corenzio. *Via S Biagio 114 • Map P2 • Open 9am–7pm Sat, 9am–2pm Sun • Free*

6 Santa Maria Maggiore

Nicknamed *Pietrasanta* (holy stone) after its ancient stone marked with a cross, thought to grant indulgences to whoever kissed it, the original church here was built in the 10th and 11th centuries and the belltower is Naples' only example of early medieval architecture. The present church, however, is Baroque. ✆ *Via dei Tribunali • Map N2 • Closed for restoration*

7 Pio Monte della Misericordia

This charitable institution was founded in 1601, inspired by Counter-Reformation precepts which gave weight to such works as a way of ensuring salvation. The church is set back from the street by a five-arch loggia, where pilgrims could find shelter. The altarpiece, *The Acts of Mercy* by Caravaggio, is a snapshot of a Neapolitan street in the 17th century. ✆ *Via dei Tribunali 253 • Map Q2 • Open 9am–1pm Mon–Sat • Free*

8 Santa Lucia

According to legend, a church dedicated to St Lucy was built here in ancient times, although most experts date the earliest structure to the 9th century. Destroyed and rebuilt repeatedly, the present church is postwar. All the artworks were destroyed in World War II bombings, save an 18th-century statue of St Lucy and a couple of paintings. ✆ *Via Sta Lucia 3 • Map N6 • Open 7am–noon, 5–7pm Mon–Sat, 8am–1pm, 5–7pm Sun • Free*

9 San Pietro ad Aram

Tradition holds that St Peter celebrated his first mass in Naples here, although historians claim the church is 12th-century. ✆ *Corso Umberto I 192 • Map R2 • Open 7–10:30am, 5–7pm Mon–Wed, Fri–Sat; 7–10:30am Thu; 7am–1pm, 5–7pm Sun • Free*

Santa Lucia

10 Santa Maria del Parto

The Neapolitan poet Jacopo Sannazaro, a confirmed humanist, ordered this church to be built in the 16th century and his tomb behind the high altar is notable for its lack of Christian symbolism. In a side chapel the painting of the Archangel Michael spearing the "Mergellina Devil" records the spiritual victory of a local bishop when a woman proclaimed her love for him. ✆ *Via Mergellina 21 • Map K2 • Open 5:30–8pm Mon–Sat, 9:30am–1pm, 6–8pm Sun • Free*

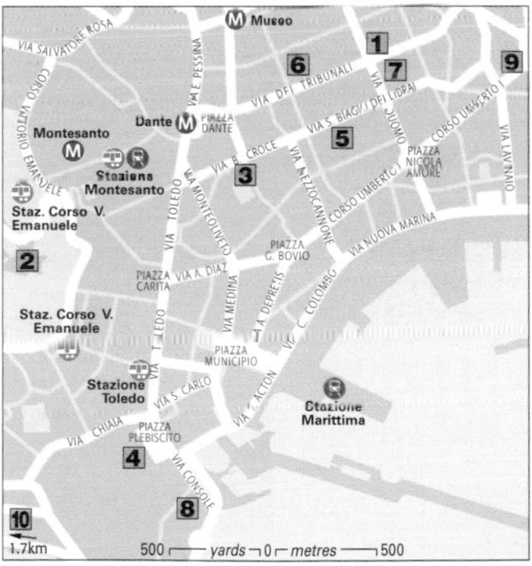

Left **Piazza Plebiscito** Right **Piazza Bellini**

TOP 10 Piazzas and Fountains

1 Piazza Plebiscito, Naples

In recent years this vast, magnificent urban space has been restored to its original grandeur. On one side is the church of San Francesco di Paola *(see p81)*, and on the other the Palazzo Reale *(see pp8–9)*. The royal equestrian statues on the square are all the work of Canova. *Map M5*

2 Fontana di Nettuna, Naples

Shifted from its long-time home at Piazza Bovio in 2001, the beautiful Fountain of Neptune now graces a wide spot on Via Medina. The 16th-century masterpiece is the work of three artists, including Pietro Bernini. *Map P4*

3 Fontana dell'Immacolatella, Naples

Composed of three triumphal arches, this Santa Lucia district landmark once adorned the Palazzo Reale. It dates from 1601 and is another creation of Pietro Bernini, as well as Michelangelo Naccherino. This grand fountain stands at one end of the seafront Lungomare *(see p48)*, while the Sebeto Fountain, a later work by Cosimo Fanzago, marks the other terminus. *Via Partenope, near Castel dell'Ovo • Map K2*

Fontana dell'Immacolatella

4 Piazza Dante, Naples

Following Italian Unification, a statue of the poet Dante was placed in the centre of the broad curve of this square which was accordingly renamed. Before that, the area was known as Largo del Mercatello, when it was a major marketplace. Today it is still a busy focal point of the old part of the city. *Map N2*

5 Piazza Bellini, Naples

Without a doubt, this is central Naples' most inviting square. With café tables lined up on the sunny side and elegant architecture facing all around, it's a favourite spot for intellectuals, artists, students and anyone who wants to take a break *(see p70)*.

6 Piazza Sannazzaro, Naples

The nautical theme of the mermaid and turtles fountain here is appropriate, as the nearby port is the main one for embarking on a trip to the islands of Capri, Ischia or Procida. *Map K2*

7 La Piazzetta, Capri

Magnetic at any time of day or night, this is Capri's most frequented spot. Marked by the little domed belltower, it has several cafés with tables outside, surrounded by whitewashed arcades *(see p28)*.

Piazza Sedile Dominova

8 Piazza Sedile Dominova, Sorrento

This Sorrento square is noteworthy for the 15th-century building from which it takes its name. The edifice was an open-air meeting place for the local aristocracy under the Angevin rulers and the fine arcaded loggia, partially enclosed by balustrades, still preserves some faded frescoes and a majolica dome. These days, the structure is the focus of the local working men's club. ✎ *Map D5*

9 Piazza Duomo, Amalfi

Dominated by the steps up to the cathedral and the black-and-white design of the building and its belltower, this square is a hub of café life. ✎ *Map E5*

10 Piazza Duomo, Ravello

Any visit to Ravello will begin and end in this charming piazza, so perhaps most significant are the several choices of direction you can take from here. Staircases and ramped walkways lead off in all directions around the town. ✎ *Map E4*

Top 10 Parks and Gardens

1 Santi Marcellino e Festo Cloister, Naples

The site of former 8th-century monasteries enjoys fine views. ✎ *Largo S Marcellino 10 • Map P3 • Open 8am–8pm Mon–Fri, 8am–2pm Sat • Free*

2 Orto Botanico, Naples

The "Royal Plant Garden" was founded by Joseph Bonaparte in 1807 *(see p70)*.

3 Capodimonte, Naples

Established by Charles III, this park has numerous ancient trees *(see pp18–19)*.

4 Villa La Floridiana, Naples

These grounds have been a public park since the 1920s *(see p52)*. ✎ *Map J4*

5 Villa Comunale, Naples

This park is now appreciated for its statuary and fine structures *(see p82)*.

6 Parco Virgiliano, Naples

This hilltop position provides fine panoramas *(see p109)*.

7 Caserta Park, Naples

These 18th-century gardens were influenced by Versailles *(see p111)*.

8 La Mortella, Ischia

Ischia's fabulous gardens include rare species. ✎ *Via F Calise 35, Forio • Map A4 • Open Apr–mid-Nov: 9am–8pm Tue, Thu, Sat–Sun • Adm*

9 Gardens of Augustus, Capri

The island's primary green spot. ✎ *Via Matteotti • Map C5 • Open dawn–dusk daily • Free*

10 Villa Cimbrone, Ravello

Some say the view from here is the most beautiful in the world *(see p30)*.

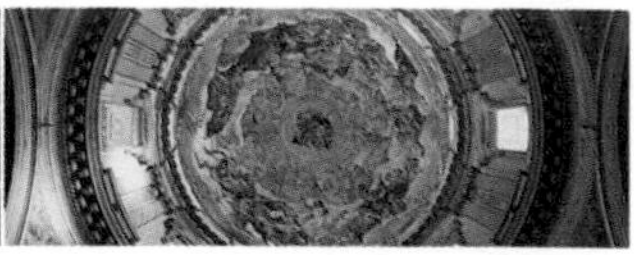

Left **Drunken Silenus, Ribera** Right **Cappella di San Gennaro fresco, Domenichino**

TOP 10 Artists and their Masterpieces

1 Pietro Cavallini

Many scholars now credit this Roman artist (c.1250–c.1330) with much of the St Francis fresco in Assisi, until recently attributed to Giotto. His work in Naples includes *Scenes from the Lives of Christ and John the Baptist* in San Domenico Maggiore *(see p74)*.

2 Donatello

The *bas-relief* of the Assumption, the cardinal's head and the caryatid on the right of the Tomb of Cardinal Rinaldo Brancaccio in Sant'Angelo a Nilo church *(see p74)* are assumed to be the only pieces in Naples by this Florentine master (1386–1466).

3 Masaccio

A 15th-century *Crucifixion* by this Tuscan painter (1401–28) is one of the treasures of the Capodimonte Museum. The work is a blend of the formal medieval tradition and the vitality of the Renaissance. Of note are the anatomical accuracy of Christ's torso and the sense of drama created by the outstretched arms of Mary Magdalene.

Madonna with Child and Two Angels, Botticelli

4 Sandro Botticelli

Typical of this much-loved Florentine artist (1444–1510) is his *Madonna with Child and Two Angels* in the Capodimonte Museum. Although it is an early work, all of the hallmarks of the painter at his height are here: the delicacy of the veils; the refinement of features; and the soulful eyes, evoking sublimity.

5 Titian

This consummate painter of the Venetian Renaissance (c.1490–1576) is represented in Naples by several works, all but one in the Capodimonte Museum. These include his sensuous masterpiece *Danaë*, and the religious works *La Maddalena* and *Annunciazione*.

6 Caravaggio

This Baroque master (1571–1610) created a lasting artistic revolution with his dramatic use of *chiaroscuro* (light and shade). He spent a year or so in Naples; among the works he completed here is *Flagellation of Christ*, originally in the San Domenico Maggiore church but now in Capodimonte.

Flagellation of Christ, Caravaggio

7 Domenichino
A mammoth fresco cycle by this painter (1581–1641) adorns the Duomo's Cappella di San Gennaro *(see p12)*, depicting episodes from the life of Naples' patron saint.

8 Jusepe Ribera
The Spanish painter (1590–1652) spent much of his life in Naples, where he created powerful and original works. These include his *San Sebastiano* in the Certosa di San Martino *(see p22)*.

9 Artemisia Gentileschi
It is said that Gentileschi (1597–1652) was violated in her youth and brought the pain of her indignation to her astounding *Judith and Holofernes*, now in Capodimonte. She was virtually the only female artist of the age to rise to fame.

10 Luca Giordano
One of the most prolific of Naples' Baroque artists (1632–1705). His paintings and frescoes are ubiquitous in the city, adorning churches and museums. Most significant is *Triumph of Judith* on the Treasury ceiling in the Certosa di San Martino *(see pp20–23)*.

Top 10 Writers and Philosophers

1 Virgil
The epic poet (70–19 BC) lived in Naples for many years, incorporating local legends into his work *The Aeneid*.

2 Petronius
In his saga *The Satyricon*, only a fragment of which survives, this author (d.AD 66) captures the decadence of the Roman Empire in the villas of Naples.

3 Pliny the Younger
Thanks to this writer (AD 62–113) we know much about the day Vesuvius erupted and buried Pompeii *(see p27)*.

4 Suetonius
The writer (69–140) is famous for his *Twelve Caesars*, scandalous accounts of the first Roman emperors.

5 St Thomas Aquinas
The theologian (1225–74) was often a guest at San Domenico Maggiore, headquarters for religious study at the University of Naples.

6 Petrarch
The great lyric poet and scholar (1304–74) often visited the court of Robert of Anjou in Naples.

7 Giovanni Boccaccio
Author of *The Decameron* (1348–53), 10 tales of ribaldry in medieval Naples.

8 Torquato Tasso
An epic poet and a native of Sorrento (1544–95).

9 Giovanni Battista Vico
Born in Naples in 1668, Vico found fame with his influential *La Scienza Nuova (The New Science)* (1725).

10 Benedetto Croce
The philosopher, historian and statesman (1866–1952) spent much time in Naples.

Left **Totò** Right **Massimo Troisi in Il Postino**

Top 10 Icons of Popular Culture

Pulcinella

1 Pulcinella

Cunning, perpetually hungry and rambunctious, *Pulcinella* (Little Chicken) is the symbol of Neapolitans and their streetwise way of life. His signature white pyjama-like outfit, peaked hat and hook-nosed mask go back to ancient Roman burlesque, in which a bawdy clown, Macchus, was one of the stock characters. He is the prototype of Punch and similar anarchic puppets around the world.

2 Scugnizzi and Lazzaroni

These two characters, products of the poverty the city has historically suffered, are street urchins and ruffians. Both have been heavily romanticized by outsiders, yet their sly wisdom and wit are traits all Neapolitans seem to aspire to.

3 Presepi

The tradition of creating sculpted tableaux of Christ's birth *(presepi)* has risen to a high art in Naples ever since the 1700s. Sculptors create scenes that expand far beyond the central event and include features of everyday life – Pulcinella may be shown slapping the current mayor, for example.

4 Neapolitan Song

Naples has always been known as a city of music, with songs focusing nostalgically on love, the sun and the sea. *O' Sole Mio* and *Santa Lucia* are the most renowned. Of the top musicians, Pino Daniele has gained the greatest fame outside Italy.

5 Totò

For many, this rubber-faced comedian was the quintessence of Italian humour. Until his death in 1967, "The Prince of Laughter" made five films a year, some of them comic masterpieces. One of his most successful was *Un Turco Napoletano* (A Neapolitan Turk, 1953).

6 Eduardo De Filippo

De Filippo (1900–84) combined the roles of comic actor, manager and playwright. His comedies, originally in the Neapolitan dialect, revolve around the petty concerns of family life and were performed by his family troupe. His best known film is *Napoli Milionaria* (1950).

Sophia Loren

7 Sophia Loren
An indefatigable love goddess since her star began to rise in 1954 in *L'Oro di Napoli (The Gold of Naples)*, "La Loren" went on to become a Hollywood star.

8 Massimo Troisi
Embodying the heart of the Neapolitan character, this actor made international waves with *Il Postino (The Postman)*, nominated for an Academy Award in 1995. Sadly, after the film was completed, Troisi died at the age of 41.

9 Naples in the Movies
Greats of the golden age of Italian cinema all felt inspired to communicate their impressions of Naples. Notable films include Roberto Rossellini's *Viaggio in Italia* (1953) and Francesco Rossi's *Mani Sulla Città* (1963).

10 Recent International Films
Naples and the coast have provided the setting for films as diverse as the fifth *Star Wars* installment, which used the Royal Palace at Caserta for the queen's abode, and *The Talented Mr Ripley*, wherein the protagonists soak up the sun in a beach town near the city.

Top 10 Opera Legends

1 Teatro San Carlo
The oldest working opera theatre in Europe, 40 years older than Milan's La Scala *(see p82)*.

2 Inauguration
On 4 November 1737 the San Carlo was inaugurated with Metastasio's opera *Achille in Sciro*.

3 Castrati
An 18th-century Neapolitan speciality, renowned *castrati* who sang at the San Carlo included Caffarelli (Gaetano Majorano), Farinelli (Carlo Broschi) and Gian Battista Velluti.

4 Fire
In February 1816 fire destroyed the San Carlo. In a few months the theatre had been rebuilt with perfect acoustics.

5 Ballet
San Carlo shares with La Scala the record for the first Italian ballet school (1812).

6 Gioacchino Rossini
The composer wrote some 50 operas and was artistic director of the opera house between 1815 and 1822.

7 Gaetano Donizetti
Donizetti composed 16 operas for the San Carlo, including *Lucia di Lammermoor*.

8 Vincenzo Bellini
In 1826 Bellini was asked to stage his first work at the San Carlo, *Bianca e Gerlando*.

9 Giuseppe Verdi
The "god" of Italian opera wrote his first opera for the theatre, *Alzira*, in 1845.

10 Non-Singing Celebrities
A recent development is for stars such as Vanessa Redgrave and Gérard Depardieu to perform in non-singing roles.

Left **Lungomare** Right **Vesuvius**

TOP 10 Walks

1 Spaccanapoli

The colloquial name of this ancient street means "Splits Naples", which is exactly what it does, cutting the oldest part of the city right down the middle. Beginning at the western end in Piazza del Gesù Nuovo, a straight line takes you past some of the city's finest monuments. In addition, there are shops, bars, cafés and pizzerias *(see pp68–79)*.

2 Decumano Maggiore

In Roman times this street, now known as Via dei Tribunali, was the main east-west artery of the city. It constitutes the heart of the old quarter and is replete with unmissable sights, as well as intriguing shops and bars and cafés to while away the hours. *Map P2*

3 Royal Naples

For regal edifices, including castles and palaces and elegant cafés and shops, this is a choice part of town and recently renovated to be more pedestrian-friendly. A good place to start is at the Fontana di Nettuno on Via Medina *(see p42)* and then head down towards the sea and west. This arc will take in many highlights, including Castel Nuovo, Teatro San Carlo and Galleria Umberto I. *Map P4*

Royal Naples

4 Lungomare

Beginning at the public gardens next to the Palazzo Reale, take the seaside road around the Santa Lucia quarter and past some of Naples' loveliest areas, including the island of Castel dell'Ovo and the green splendour of the Villa Comunale. *Map N6*

5 Via Toledo

From the royal quarter Via Toledo begins elegantly, but soon the *Quartieri Spagnoli* (Spanish Quarters) come up along the western flank – a warren of narrow, dark streets that don't seem to have changed in centuries. However, continuing on you'll pass appealing Piazza Dante and finally come to the Museo Archeologico. *Map N3*

6 Vesuvius

A walk along the rim of this vast crater is an experience of a lifetime. Some 20,000 visitors a year trek to the top to peer down into the steaming depths 200 m (700 ft) below. The hike up takes 45 minutes and it's at its best in late spring, when flowers and songbirds are most vibrant *(see p89)*.

7 Sorrentine Peninsula

If you take the *funivia* (cable-car) from Castellammare di Stabia up to Monte Faito there are startling views from the top, as well as the beginning of numerous nature trails, some of which eventually lead as far as Positano. *Map E4*

8 The Amalfi Coast

Excellent hiking points can be reached above Positano and between Ravello and Amalfi-Atrani. Most of these paths are erstwhile goat trails, while some have been built up as stone stairways, but all of them offer incomparable views *(see p97)*.

9 Capri

Once you get away from the smart shops and hotels, this island is all about nature walks: up to Villa Jovis, down to the Arco Naturale, through the forest to the Blue Grotto – the possibilities are numerous *(see pp28–9)*.

10 Ischia

The walks and hikes on this island are plentiful. A memorable trek is up Monte Epomeo from Forio, through Fontana, taking about 40 minutes *(see p96)*.

Top 10 Drives

1 The Phlegrean Fields
Hug the coastline from Posillipo to Pozzuoli and take local roads to Agnano Terme and La Solfatara. *Map J2*

2 Cumae
Begin at Lago d'Averno and pass under the Arco Felice to arrive at the ancient site of Cumae. *Map B3*

3 Naples to Sorrento
Driving on the tollway can be very stressful, but once you cut off to Castellammare di Stabia, there's only one picturesque road. *Map E4*

4 Sorrento to Positano
Follow the signs to Santa Agata sui Due Golfi and then Colli di Fontanelle. Eventually, you will get your first glimpse of Positano. *Map D5*

5 Positano to Vietri
A single road "of 1,000 turns" winds along this spectacular coast. *Map E5*

6 Amalfi to Ravello
Leave the coast road and climb up and up for a vista unlike any other. *Map E5*

7 Around Ischia
A fairly good road rings the island. *Map B4*

8 Marina Grande to Anacapri, Capri
This breathtaking cliff road is best experienced in one of the island's classic open-top taxis. *Map U1*

9 Naples to Caserta
Getting up to this northern palace will test your driving skills to the max but the end result is rewarding. *Map D1*

10 Naples to Paestum
Take the A3 or the N18 to Salerno, then switch to the N19, direction Battipaglia. Take the right fork for Paestum, the N18 south. *Map H6*

***Note:** No private cars are allowed on the island of Capri, but buses and taxis are readily available.*

Left **Marina di Praia** Right **Marina Piccola, Capri**

Top 10 Beaches

1 Posillipo & Beyond

The nearest beaches to the centre of Naples that are of any appeal can be found at Posillipo, although they're shingle, not sand, and the water is far from immaculate. Further away, at the ends of the Cumana and Circumflegrea railways, there are more attractive sandy beaches, although, again, they are not especially pristine.
Map J2

Posillipo beach

2 Procida

This small island has several good beach options. One of the longest stretches from Chiaiolella Marina to Ciriaccio; called the Lido, it is the island's most popular beach so expect crowds. From here a bridge leads to the nature reserve of Vivara, which has rocky access to the sea. To the northeast, Pozzo Vecchio also has a beach *(see p96)*.

3 Ischia

To gain access to any beach here – at least the good parts – you will need to pay, but for around €15 to €20 per day you receive the use of a sunbed and an umbrella. There are plenty of beaches to choose from, including sandy stretches in Forio and Ischia Porto. More out-of-the-way options include San Montano and Sorgeto *(see p96)*.

4 Capri

There's very little in the way of sandy beaches here, although there is a small one just up from Marina Grande. A popular pebbly choice is Marina Piccola, where there are full facilities including some good restaurants. The more adventurous should head down to the bottom of Via Krupp, where huge flat stones lie along the shore *(see pp28–9)*.

5 Sorrento

In this resort town bathing platforms have been constructed, with lifts or steps leading down to them from several hotels, but unless you are a hotel resident

Sorrento

you will have to pay for this option. Elsewhere along the peninsula there's a fine beach to the east, at Meta di Sorrento, while to the west, there's a small sandy beach at Marina di Puolo and another at Marina di Lobra *(see p96)*.

6 Positano
Again, at this fashionable, busy resort, payment is necessary for a sunbed and umbrella. For something a little more independent take the path to the west, around the cliff, to the beach at Fornillo – it's smaller and rockier but more relaxed *(see p100)*.

7 Marina di Praia
This small cove, just beyond Positano, has a bit of beach you can generally call your own, as few tourists stop here. However you will share the cove with local fishing boats, a couple of bar-restaurants, a diving centre and the coast's premier disco, Africana *(see p100)*.

8 Marina di Furore
A very precipitous path goes straight down to this tiny beach. A few fishermen's homes cluster here, with their boats neatly moored along one side, and there's a bar-restaurant. *Map E5*

9 Minori & Maiori
These two towns are home to the Amalfi Coast's longest and flattest beaches, now developed into rather low-key tourist resorts *(see p100)*.

10 Erchie & Cetara
The beach at Erchie is a small cove graced by a watch-tower, fishing boats and a few houses. At Cetara bathers share the narrow rocky strip with boats, but it's good for a dip. *Map F4*

Top 10 Spas

1 Terme di Agnano
A spa since ancient times. Mud-baths and mineral waters. *Via Agnano Astroni 24, Naples • Map J2*

2 Giardini Poseidon, Ischia
Saunas, Jacuzzis, pools and treatments. *Via Mazzella • Map A4*

3 Negombo, Ischia
Beautiful gardens and volcanic springs. *Via Baia di S Montano, Lacco Ameno • Map A4*

4 Parco Termale Aphrodite Apollon, Ischia
Pools, saunas and massage. *Via Petrelle, Sant'Angelo • Map A4*

5 Terme Belliazzi, Ischia
Mud treatments and massage. *Piazza Bagni 134, Casamicciola • Map A4*

6 Terme di Cava Scura, Ischia
Built into the cliffs, with a cave sauna and baths in sulphurous water. *Via Cava Scura, Serrara Fontana • Map A4*

7 Terme della Regina Isabella, Ischia
Luxury massage and treatments. *Piazza Sta Restituta, Lacco Ameno • Map A4*

8 Capri Palace Hotel
Anacapri's top hotel also has a spa and beauty treatment centre *(see p128)*.

9 Hotel Capo La Gala, Vico Equense
Enjoy a swimming pool filled with natural mineral water. *Via Luigi Serio 8 • Map D4*

10 Terme di Stabia, Castellammare di Stabia
Mud, mineral waters and massage. *Viale delle Terme 3–5 • Map E4*

For more details on spas in Ischia visit www.ischiaonline.com

Left **Villa La Floridiana** Right **Gardens of Villa Cimbrone**

Top 10 Romantic Spots

1 Villa La Floridiana, Naples

Lucia Migliaccio, Duchess of Floridia, once called this sumptuous place home – a love token from her husband, Ferdinand I, whose morganatic wife she became soon after the death of his first wife, Maria Carolina of Austria. Not only is the story romantic but the situation itself affords some of the finest views of the city and the bay. The gardens are good for hours of peaceful strolling, and the main building is now a museum filled with delightful treasures *(see p43)*. *Via Domenico Cimarosa 77 • Map J4 • Open 9am–1hr before sunset*

2 Marechiaro

This little fishing village between the tip of Capo di Posillipo and Punta del Cavallo is famous with locals for its time-tested romantic atmosphere. The vista from here is said to be so gorgeous that even the fish come here to woo their sweethearts, especially by the light of the moon. There are a number of excellent and inviting restaurants clustered around the prime viewing spot, all specializing in fish, of course *(see p109)*.

3 D'Angelo Santa Caterina Restaurant, Naples

For special events of any kind, you can't do better than this. The food is excellent, focusing on a rich assortment of seafood *antipasti* notable for its delicate finesse, while the views are sublime, taking in the sweep of the entire bay. Be sure to commandeer a terrace table; the striped canopies and delightful multicoloured tile floor create an irresistibly charming impression. *Via Aniello Falcone 203 • Map J4 • 081 578 97 72 • Closed L, Tue, 2 weeks Aug • €€€€€*

4 Le Grotelle Restaurant, Capri

The cuisine here is simple, homemade fare that includes seafood, fish, pasta, chicken and perhaps rabbit, while the wine is local and very creditable. What makes it so romantic is the unsurpassed setting. Not only is it close to nature, being situated almost all the way down to the Arco Naturale, but the terrace tables also enjoy an eye-popping view straight down to the sea, along a precipitous ravine. In addition, the friendly owners do their best to make any meal a memorable event. *Via Arco Naturale • Map U1 • 081 837 57 19 • Closed May, Jun & Sep: Thu; Apr & Oct: D; Nov–Mar • €€*

Le Grotelle Restaurant

For a guide to restaurant prices **See p79**

Terrace, Hotel Caesar Augustus

5 Blue Grotto, Capri

So beautiful is the radiant aquamarine that glows upwards from inside this cave that it is truly indescribable. As you are ferried through the tiny entrance by a boatman you will find complete serenity *(see p29)*.

6 Villa Eva Resort, Anacapri

Set amid sub-tropical gardens, this resort consists of a main house and bungalows. Each accommodation is unique and there's also a wonderful grand piano shaped swimming pool *(see p128)*.

Ferry boat, Blue Grotto

7 Hotel Caesar Augustus, Anacapri

Recently upgraded to luxury class, the big pull at this hotel remains its terrace, touted as the most beautiful panorama in the world. In one sweep it takes in the entire bay *(see p128)*.

8 Villa Maria Restaurant, Ravello

Such a beautiful view from the vine-covered garden deserves superb food, and that is just what you find here. The restaurant, part of the Hotel Villa Maria *(see p130)*, is one of Ravello's best. A signature dish is prawns and smoked cheese grilled on skewers; for a sweet finish, try the incredible lemon mousse.

Via Sta Chiara 2 • Map E4 • 089 85 72 55 • Dis. access • €€€

9 Villa Cimbrone Gardens, Ravello

Greta Garbo enjoyed her love affair with the conductor Arturo Toscanini in this beautiful spot, declared by resident American writer Gore Vidal to be one of the most beautiful places on earth. Wander the many maze-like plantings and terraced levels filled with hidden treasures and beautiful statues *(see p30)*.

10 Paestum

Most evocative at dawn or sunset, when it is possible to imagine what the ancient city might have been like, these Greek temples and their verdant setting are a reminder of all that is loveliest in life. Spend the day here to explore these remains of one of history's most evolved cultures *(see pp32–3)*.

Left **San Severo Catacombs** Right **Green Grotto**

Top 10 Hidden Attractions

1 Napoli Sotterranea
This tour's entrance is next to San Paolo Maggiore *(see p74)* and takes you into a world of excavations that date back to the 4th century BC. The digging began when the Greeks quarried large tufa blocks to build the city of Neapolis. Caves were also dug here to be used as tombs. Centuries later the Romans turned this underground area into aqueducts and cisterns, which were in use until the cholera epidemic of 1884. *Piazza S Gaetano 68 • Map P2 • Guided tours: noon, 2pm & 4pm Mon–Fri (& 9pm Thu); 10am, noon, 2pm, 4pm & 6pm Sat–Sun • Adm*

2 San Severo Catacombs
Naples' first bishop was buried here in the 4th century and, as was customary, a large underground cemetery grew up around his tomb. Among the catacombs' paintings is a fresco showing the earliest images in Naples of saints Peter and Paul. *Piazzetta S Severo a Capodimonte 81 • Map K1 • 081 544 13 05 • Open by appt only • Donation*

3 San Gaudioso Catacombs
This labyrinth of tunnels was built by the Romans for use as cisterns. It evolved into catacombs in the 5th century, when St Gaudiosus, a North African bishop and hermit, was interred here. You can see the remains of fresco and mosaic decorations. *Basilica of Sta Maria alla Sanità, Via della Sanità 124 • Map K1 • Guided tours: 9:30am, 10:15am, 11am, 11:45am & 12:30pm daily (& 5:10pm, 5:50pm, 6:30pm Sat) • Adm*

4 Cimitero delle Fontanelle
Once a Roman quarry for tufa blocks, this cavern became a gruesome depository for the city's dead during the cholera epidemic of 1884. Graves and tombs were emptied all over Naples and the skulls stacked here – some 40,000 in all, with the addition of still more during the cholera outbreak of 1974. *Via delle Fontanelle 154 • Map K1 • 081 29 69 44 • Open by appt only*

5 San Gennaro Catacombs
Burials here date as far back as the 2nd century and the site was originally used by pagans as well as Christians. In the 5th century, the body of San

San Gennaro Catacombs

The faint-hearted may find the Cimitero delle Fontanelle disturbing, particularly younger children.

Gennaro, Naples' patron saint, was brought here, and the place became an important pilgrimage site. Frescoes and mosaics on the two levels of this vast layout attest to its importance over the centuries. *Via Capodimonte 16 • Map K1 • Guided tours: 9:30am, 10:15am, 11am & 11:45am daily • Adm*

6 Tomb of Virgil and Crypta Neapolitana

What is known as Virgil's tomb is a Roman burial vault that dates back to the Augustan age. It is a typical *columbarium*, the "dove-cote" style of burial, with niches for urns containing the ashes of the deceased. The Romans later took to burying their dead in *sarcophagi* (coffins), as the fashion changed to belief in an afterlife, perhaps adopted from the Egyptians. Next to the tomb are a tufa quarry and a *crypta* (tunnel), built as an underground road in the 1st century. *Salita della Grotta 20, Mergellina • Map K2 • Open 9am–1hr before sunset daily • Free*

7 Città Sommersa, Baia

Most of the ancient city of Baia now lies underwater, due to the shifting of the coastline and slow seismic disturbances. What you can still make out just below the surface of the water, however, are remnants of the grandiose port and parts of various villas and temples *(see p110)*. *Piazza della Repubblica 42 • Map B3 • Guided tours mid-Mar–early Nov: noon & 4pm Sat; 10:30am, noon & 4pm Sun • Adm*

8 Sibyl's Grotto, Cumae

Although some experts believe that this magnificent structure served a military purpose in Roman times, others hold with a mythological origin. Walking along the unusual wedge-shaped walls, pierced at intervals with shafts of light, creates a decidedly hypnotic effect on most visitors, as if in preparation for an encounter with the great oracle herself in her grotto *(see p111)*.

Sibyl's Grotto

9 Green Grotto, Capri

Located on the other side of the island from its far more famous sibling, the Blue Grotto *(see p29)*, this smaller cave glows emerald green once you duck inside. The best way to get here is to rent a kayak at Punta Carena and then make your way past Marina Piccola towards the Faraglioni rocks. *Map U2*

10 Spiaggia del Fornillo, Positano

Few know that there's a pleasant alternative to the crowded main beach at Positano, with its rows of sunbeds and umbrellas. To get to Fornillo, head west on the path past the 'O Guarracino restaurant, around the cliff. It's a rocky beach, overlooked by two towers, but there's a café-restaurant and facilities *(see p51)*.

Left **Villa Comunale** Right **Marina Piccola Beach**

TOP 10 Children's Attractions

1 Villa Comunale

This major urban park in central Naples has a playground specifically designed with little ones in mind and there are always plenty of families enjoying the gardens and walkways. Vendors also hawk all sorts of festive toys that kids love. The biggest attraction for youngsters may be the Stazione Zoologica (Zoological Institute), featuring sea life from the Bay of Naples *(see p82)*.

Science City

2 Science City

A hands-on, interactive "experimentorium", with something for everyone, even the very young. Included in the exhibits are a planetarium as well as up-to-date computer gizmos, all of which seem to transcend language barriers *(see p112)*.

3 Edenlandia

This traditional amusement park might be showing its age a bit and isn't giving Disney any competition, but kids of all ages will find plenty to enjoy. Rides include a Big Dipper, a Ghost Train, a Canoe Flume and Bumper Cars, as well as several more high-tech options. A low-tech, old-fashioned choice that never fails to delight is Le Nuvole, a theatre group that features puppets and mime.
Viale Kennedy, Fuorigrotta • Map J2 • Open Apr–May: 2–8pm Tue–Fri, 10:30am–midnight Sat–Sun; Jun–Sep: 5pm–midnight Mon–Fri, 10:30am–midnight Sat–Sun; Oct–Mar: 10:30am–midnight Sat–Sun • Adm

4 Musei Interdipartimentali

Four museums in one are housed in the Università di Napoli Federico II. Rockhounds will love the Mineralogy and Geology Museum; the Anthropology Museum is fascinating; animal lovers will relate to the Zoology Museum; and the Palaeontology Museum has dinosaur exhibits.
Via Mezzocannone 8 & Largo S Marcellino 10 • Map P3 • Open 9am–1:30pm, 3–5pm Mon; 9am–1:30pm Tue–Fri; 9am–1pm Sat–Sun • Adm

5 Ospedale delle Bambole

Children are captivated by the Doll Hospital, both for the concept as well as for the array of dolls that are here to be "cured". Adults, too, will find the collection fascinating, with some pieces qualifying as museum-quality treasures. The place is a shop as well, so your child won't necessarily have to say goodbye to a new-found friend at the end of the visit. *Via S Biagio dei Librai 81 • Map P2 • Open 10am–5pm Mon–Fri • Free*

For tips on travelling as a family **See p122**

Funicular Railway

6 Funicular Railways

With all the hills in the area, both in Naples and around the bay, these fun people-movers have proved a charming necessity. The most accessible and important ones, that inspired the rousing ditty *"Funicolì, funicolà"*, are those that take you from the historic centre up to Vomero.

7 Pietrarsa Railway Museum

The first railway in the area was inaugurated by King Ferdinand II in 1839 and 150 years later the railway workshop was opened as a museum. It's the largest of its kind in Europe and has impressive displays, including a magnificent reconstruction of the first royal train here and a line-up of later carriages, many of them lavishly gilded. *Via Pietrarsa, Portici • Map D3 • Open 9am–1pm Mon–Sat • Free*

8 Vesuvius

No child will ever forget a trip up the cone of this killer volcano and a peek over the rim into the steaming abyss far below. It's a fairly easy walk – only about half an hour – and the thrill will stay with them for years *(see p89)*.

9 Solfatara

Another phenomenal geothermal playground that will fascinate budding geologists. This congealed lava cap plugging up a dormant volcano is an expanse of hissing, fuming, bubbling terrain like nothing you will have seen before. There's also a campsite with restaurant right on the spot – you get used to the sulphur smell in a day or two *(see p112)*.

10 Marina Piccola Beach, Capri

One of the most child-friendly beaches in the area: the water is tranquil and the bathing areas well protected. For all the water toys and gear you might require, as well as sunscreen, there are lots of shops handy, and a wide choice of places to eat. Changing rooms, umbrellas and sunbeds are available, too *(see p29)*.

Climbing Vesuvius

Left **Snorkelling** Right **Boating**

TOP 10 Sporting Activities

1 Swimming
The best places for swimming in the sea are away from Naples proper, either at beaches and coves on the islands or along the coast around Sorrento and Amalfi *(see pp50–51)*.

2 Diving and Snorkelling
The islands have diving centres, as do parts of the Amalfi Coast, where courses are available and you can rent or buy any equipment you might need. Some organize night dives and marine nature dives for the experienced. Otherwise, rent or buy a mask, snorkel and a pair of flippers and paddle about to your heart's content; there's plenty to see just under the surface in the quieter coves and tide pools.
Roja Diving Center: Hotel Conte, Via Nazario Sauro 54, Sant'Angelo, Ischia; 081 99 92 14 • Procida Diving Centre: Lungomare Cristoforo Colombo 6, Lido di Procida; 081 896 83 85 • Centro Sub Costiera Amalfitana: Via Fornillo, Positano; 089 81 21 48

3 Kayaking
Circumnavigating Capri *(see pp28–9)* in one of these tiny pleasure canoes (1- or 2-person) is an unforgettable experience, taking about five hours if you stop to check out the occasional grotto or go for a swim. A treat is sailing through the arched hole in the largest *faraglioni* rock, but make sure no power boats are doing it at the same time, or you might be swamped.

4 Windsurfing and Boating
Windsurfing gear can be rented at the more frequented beaches on the islands and along the outlying coasts; the Lido of Procida is good, as well as Punta Carena on Capri. Renting boats and yachts is possible on the islands and along the Amalfi Coast but again, Procida is the best spot. *Sailitalia Procida: Via Roma 10, Marina Grande, Procida; 081 896 99 62; www.sailitalia.com*

5 Jogging and In-Line Skating
The parks in Naples are best for jogging, primarily Villa La Floridiana *(see p43)*, which has plenty of foliage to block out direct sun. Further afield, Parco Virgiliano *(see p109)* has plenty of space for a run. For in-line skating, Naples' seafront has flat stretches.

Windsurfer

If participating in an outdoor sport in summer make sure to wear high-factor sunscreen and, where appropriate, carry bottled water.

Italian football match

6 Hiking

The islands and the Sorrentine Peninsula are liberally criss-crossed with hiking trails galore, of every degree of difficulty from a country stroll to a full day's all-out trek to unfrequented parts. Many are ancient, even prehistoric goat trails that pass by spots of timeless beauty. If you have time to work in a day of hiking while here it's well worth it for the intimate contact you will have with this beautiful landscape *(see pp48–9)*.

7 Work-Outs

Gym-culture came to Italy in the 1990s and appears to be here to stay. Top gyms in Naples offer bodybuilding, aerobics, step, martial arts and various other activities, as well as saunas and Turkish baths.

Athena: Via dei Mille 16, Chiaia; 081 40 73 34 • Bodyguard: Via Torrione San Martino 45, Vomero, 081 558 45 51

8 Tennis

Tennis is very much in favour among Italians, and there are good clay courts in Naples, as well as plenty on the islands. Some are beautifully landscaped garden spots and are floodlit at night as well. Most welcome non-members for a reasonable hourly fee and rent equipment of all kinds. Some provide rackets free of charge and will also line you up with a partner if necessary. *Tennis Club Napoli: Villa Comunale, Viale Dohrn; 081 761 46 56 • Tennis San Domenico: Via S Domenico 64, Vomero Alto; 081 46 56 60 • Tennis Lido: Via Cristoforo Colombo 2, Ischia Ponte; 081 98 52 45*

9 Football

The top spectator sport in Italy is, of course, *calcio* (football/soccer). So important is it in Naples – the city that in the days of the phenomenal Diego Maradona was number one in the world – that fans fervently pray to the city's patron saint, San Gennaro, to intercede in the score. To witness the euphoria for yourself, attend a match on alternate Sundays between September and June at Stadio San Paolo. *Stadio San Paolo: Piazzale Tecchio, Fuorigrotta; 081 593 32 23*

10 Regattas

A more picturesque body of water to hold a splendid regatta on would be hard to imagine, and this stretch of the Tyrrhenian Sea has its share. These include the Vela Longa in May, open to all sailboats, and the "Regatta of the Three Gulfs" namely Gaeta, Naples and Salerno, held in early June. Every four years the traditional "Regatta of the Maritime Republics", which include Amalfi, Genoa, Pisa and Venice, also occurs in June – the next one is scheduled for 2005. The colourful scenario generally involves each former republic sending out its galleon in mock combat, then they race alongside other craft.

Tickets for football matches in Naples are always at a premium so it is advisable to phone ahead.

Left **Antipasti** Right **Spaghetti alle vongole**

TOP 10 Neapolitan Dishes

Pizza napolitana

1 Pizza

Perhaps it's the water, or the quality of the flour or yeast used, but Neapolitan pizza is inimitable. It's spongy, chewy, succulent and melts in your mouth, while the toppings are flavourful and aromatic. Purists insist that it was invented here centuries ago and that the only true pizza is the simplest, the *margherita* – tomato, basil and mozzarella cheese, with a sprinkling of olive oil.

2 Antipasti

The first course may be marinated fish or seafood, a selection of olives and cured meats, *bruschetta* (toasted bread) with a variety of toppings or *prosciutto* (ham) with figs or melon, depending on the season. The meal could stop here and you won't have missed out on the pleasures of the Italian table.

3 Primo

This course usually means pasta or rice, but *minestre* and *zuppe* (soups) also appear in this category. Great *primi* to look for are *spaghetti alle vongole veraci* (with clams), *pasta e fagioli* (with beans), *fettucine alla puttanesca* (egg noodles with tomato, capers, black olives and red pepper) and *risotto alla pescatora* (rice with seafood).

4 Secondo

Scamorza (grilled smoked mozzarella) is always included in this part of the menu, as are omelettes. Meat dishes include *vitello* (veal), *polpette* (meatballs), *carne alla pizzaiola* (with tomato and basil sauce), *involtini* (beef or ham rolls), *agnello* (lamb) or *coniglio alla cacciatora* (rabbit stew).

5 Fish and Seafood

This category is, of course, the area's strong point. *Calamari* (squid) are a favourite, as are *cozze* (mussels) in a variety of delicious presentations. *Seppie* (cuttlefish) and *polipo* (octopus) are popular, too, stewed, fried or steamed. *Pesce all'acqua pazza* (fish in "crazy water") is a treat – fresh fish stewed in water with tomatoes, garlic and chillies.

6 Contorni

The fertility of the land around Naples is never more evident that when you taste the produce it brings forth. For *contorni* (side dishes), peppers, artichokes, aubergine (eggplant), capers, mushrooms and green beans are offered steamed or sautéed. Expect the freshness of each vegetable to have been fully retained, cooked with just a touch of garlic, tomato or lemon, and some herbs.

7 Insalata

Besides the host of fresh leaves and cherry tomatoes that end up in the wonderful salads *(insalata)* here, there are two famous cold dishes from the area. The *insalata caprese* is the essence of simplicity, relying on quality *mozzarella di bufala*, ripe tomatoes and aromatic basil. *Caponata* may include marinated aubergine (eggplant), artichoke hearts and capers, with bread chunks to soak up the flavours.

8 Formaggi

Mozzarella di bufala is the signature cheese from the area. The milk of the buffalo has a tangy quality and the cheese develops a unique smoothness. The smoked version is *provola*.

9 Dolci

Many Neapolitan desserts are inspired by their Sicilian cousins, notably *delizie*, a cream-filled cake, and *pannacotta* (cooked cream), perhaps topped with fresh fruit. In season, the melon, figs and wild strawberries are unforgettable.

10 Pastries

A *sfogliatella* (pastry filled with ricotta cheese) is a sublime way to start the day, accompanied by a cup of coffee. Other treats include *babà* (cake soaked in rum and honey) and *zeppole* (pastry filled with custard and topped with wild cherries).

Fresh figs

Top 10 Local Drinks

1 White Wine

The quality of Campania wines has risen steadily in recent years. Falanghina, Greco di Tufo and Lacryma Christi are reliable names.

2 Red Wine

Full-bodied reds come from the local Aglianico grape.

3 Liqueurs

The most famous of these is the lemon liqueur *limoncello*, delivering quite a kick.

4 Beer

All major brands are available, but a local Italian favourite is Peroni. If you want draft, ask for *alla spina*.

5 Mineral Water

Italians enjoy a huge array of mineral waters. A great choice is Ferrarelle – or for something lighter, Uliveto.

6 Digestivi

Many restaurants produce their own digestive concoctions – pure alcohol with a soothing mixture of spices and flavourings.

7 Coffee

Neapolitan-style coffee traditionally comes already sweetened, and it is generally very concentrated.

8 Soft Drinks

The usual range of choices is available, but an interesting Italian cola-type drink is Chinotto.

9 Infusioni

Camomilla (camomile) is considered to be a palliative, while other herbal teas on offer include *menta* (peppermint) and *tiglio* (lime-tree).

10 Spremute

Most bars are set up, in summer, to turn out freshly squeezed orange juice and a local version of lemonade.

Left **Artisan crafting nativity figures** Right **Ceramics**

TOP 10 Neapolitan Souvenirs

1 Coral & Cameos

The tradition of miniature carvings in stone is an ancient one – the Romans (and their Renaissance imitators) used precious and semiprecious stones, from agate to emerald, as well as layered glass. Today the tradition *(see p92)* primarily focuses on gems from the sea. Coral is prized for its rich colours and soft texture, while shells are fashioned into delicate cameos.

2 Gold

Italian artisans have been famed for centuries for their goldwork, from refined chains to elaborate table centrepieces. Neapolitan artists have inherited these traditions since ancient times and local jewellery shops attest to the beauty of their creations. All gold used is at least 18 carat and prices are comparable with those in other countries, while the quality is higher.

3 Antiques

The area remains one of the great sources for antiques; especially plentiful are Baroque and Rococo furniture, as well as Empire pieces. Antique ceramics, too, are a good buy, notably handpainted tiles.

Nativity figure

4 Gouaches

Gouache is a watercolour paint applied to heavy paper that gives a very soft yet vibrant look to the surface of a painting. In the 19th century gouache landscapes of Naples, its bay and Vesuvius were produced in great numbers and many are still available at surprisingly reasonable prices. These were the postcard souvenirs for Grand Tour visitors, and to the modern eye they evoke a sense of idyllic charm. There are also prints of the more famous scenes.

5 Nativity Figures

For centuries Naples has been internationally noted for its production of figures for nativity scenes, many produced by the very best sculptors, especially in the 18th century, and reproduced to this day by skilled artisans whose *botteghe* (workshops) line the streets of the old town. A popular secular figure, done in a variety of media, including terracotta, *papier mâché*, wood, or a combination of materials, is Pulcinella *(see p46)*. There are also all sorts of other delightful puppets, dolls and masks.

Handmade notebooks

6 Handmade Paper & Cards
Amalfi was once home to a thriving paper industry *(see p39)* and the tradition carries on here in a limited way. Neapolitan playing cards and *tarocchi* (tarot) cards are sold in Naples.

7 Copies of Antiquities
Believe it or not, souvenir stalls outside archaeological sites – notably Pompeii – can be good sources of creditable copies of famous Roman sculptures, but you'll need to pick through the junk and be prepared to bargain.

8 Ceramics
Ceramics – both copies of traditional designs and original creations – are notable in Capri, Ravello and Vietri.

9 Handmade Sandals, Capri
There are a number of cobblers on the island *(see p102)* who will make made-to-measure sandals within a matter of hours.

10 Intarsio, Sorrento
Renowned for centuries for its gorgeous *intarsio* (marquetry), Sorrento continues the tradition to this day, and some of the pieces are true works of art.

Top 10 Markets

1 La Pignasecca, Naples
One of Naples' oldest markets and as cheap as it gets. *Via Pignasecca • Map M3 • 8am–1pm daily*

2 San Pasquale, Naples
Spices and fish stalls, clothing and jewellery. *Via S Pasquale • Map K6 • 8am–2pm Mon, Wed, Fri–Sat*

3 Fiera Antiquaria Napoletana, Naples
As much junk as genuine antiques, but great fun. *Villa Comunale • Map K6 • 7am–2pm last Sun of month*

4 Atignano, Naples
Everything in the way of household items. *Piazza degli Artisti, Vomero • Map K2 • 8am–1pm Mon–Sat*

5 Poggioreale
Piles of everything here, especially shoes. *Via M di Caramanico • Map L1 • 8am–2pm Mon, Fri–Sat*

6 Posillipo
Clothing, shoes and bags. *Viale Virgilio • Map J2 • 8am–2pm Thu*

7 Resina, Ercolano
Roman "antiques". *Via Pugliano • Map L2 • 8am–1pm daily*

8 Mercato del Pulci, Poggioreale
As much trash as treasure, but you're sure to find something. *Via de Roberto • Map L1 • 8am–1pm Sun*

9 Corso Garibaldi, Naples
Naples at its grittiest, with a mind-boggling range of stuff. *Map R1 • 7am–2pm daily*

10 Coral Stalls, Anacapri
To the left of the main square are stalls selling coral jewellery. *Map T1 • 9am–5pm daily*

Most of the markets in the area are closed in August due to the summer heat.

Left **Pulcinella at Carnevale** Right **Gathered walnuts, Feast of San Giovanni**

Top 10 Religious Celebrations

1 La Befana

In Italy the festival of the Epiphany is personified by La Befana, a witch-like hag flying in on a broom who delivers gifts to good children and puts "lumps of coal" (actually sweets) in the shoes of naughty ones. *6 Jan*

2 Carnevale

The irrepressible Pulcinella *(see p46)* is lord of this ultimate blow-out in Naples, just before the austerities of Lent begin. Lasagne is the traditional dish to indulge in, and masks and partying are very much a part of this age-old celebration. Kids in particular get the chance to choose their fantasy persona and parade around in all their finery. *Feb*

3 Pasqua

In Italy, *Pasqua* (Easter Sunday) and *Pasquetta* (Easter Monday) are both important, as is the week leading up them in some towns. Good Friday processions are held around the Naples area, with an especially rich one on the island of Procida. *Pasquetta* is traditionally a day for outings – picnics, weather permitting, being a top choice to celebrate the advent of spring. Near Sant'Anastasia, 15 km (9 miles) east of Naples, a festival is held at the sanctuary of the Madonna dell'Arco. *Mar or Apr*

4 San Gennaro

On the first Sunday in May is the first of a thrice-yearly event during which the blood of Naples' patron saint – who has seen the city through earthquakes, volcanic eruptions and football championships – flows again. The miracle is received with a hysteria seldom seen in this day and age – a manifestation of age-old faith that involves flower-bedecked processions of the saint's effigy through the old quarter.

Lasagne dish, Carnevale

5 San Giovanni

The feast day of St John the Baptist also sometimes sees his blood boil – a phial of it is ensconced in the church of San Gregorio Armeno *(see p74)*. Otherwise, the saint is traditionally remembered in charmingly pagan ways, linked to the summer solstice: night bathing, magicians and the gathering of walnuts to make *nocino*, a liqueur prepared for late autumn. *24 Jun*

6 Santa Maria del Carmine

Every summer, Naples' tallest belltower is "burned" in commemoration of a legend that recounts how an icon kept here, the Madonna Bruna, saved it from being destroyed by fire. An array of fireworks are dramatically set off at the climax of the festivities *(see p74)*. *16 Jul*

7 Ferragosto
The Assumption of the Virgin Mary marks the height of the summer season, when almost every shop and restaurant is closed. Pozzuoli stages a contest of climbing a greased pole, while Positano re-enacts a landing of Saracen corsairs. *15 Aug*

8 Madonna di Piedigrotta
Once a highly elaborate affair, today the event involves a song competition and theatrical events, as well as fireworks and street parties. It all centres on a 14th-century sculpture of the Madonna and Child. *7–8 Sep*

9 l'Immacolata
Celebrating the Immaculate Conception, this festival opens the Christmas season; nativity scenes go up and the Guglia dell'Immacolata *(see p70)* becomes the focal point of pious activity. *8 Dec*

10 Natale
At Christmas the streets around San Gregorio Armeno *(see p74)* are full of shoppers looking for items to complete their nativity scenes, and there are special concerts in churches around the city. *24–5 Dec*

Christmas nativity figures on sale

Top 10 Secular Festivals

1 Benvenuta Primavera
Spring is welcomed in with street theatre and garden openings. *21–22 Mar*

2 Culture Week
For one week Italy's publicly owned museums, historic and archaeological sites are free to all. *Apr*

3 Maggio dei Monumenti
Churches and buildings usually closed to the public open their doors for one week. *May*

4 Estate a Napoli
Summer in Naples includes outdoor films, theatre and music in venues around town.

5 Concerti al Tramonto, Villa San Michele, Anacapri
This genteel villa is the venue for sunset classical concerts *(see p29)*. *May–Aug*

6 Music Festival of Villa Rufolo, Ravello
What started out in Ravello now includes concert venues up and down the Amalfi Coast *(see p31)*. *Jun–Sep*

7 Neapolis Festival
Southern Italy's largest rockfest invades the area of Bagnoli. *Jul*

8 Festival delle Ville Vesuviane
The aristocratic villas along this coast play host to classical concerts *(see p92)*. *Jul*

9 Pizzafest
A celebration of the city's most famous dish, as *pizzaioli* (pizza-makers) spin their dough. *Sep*

10 Capodanno
New Year's Eve involves merrymaking in Piazza del Plebiscito and fireworks over Castel dell'Ovo. *31 Dec*

For more details on festivals and events in Naples and the region visit www.enit.it

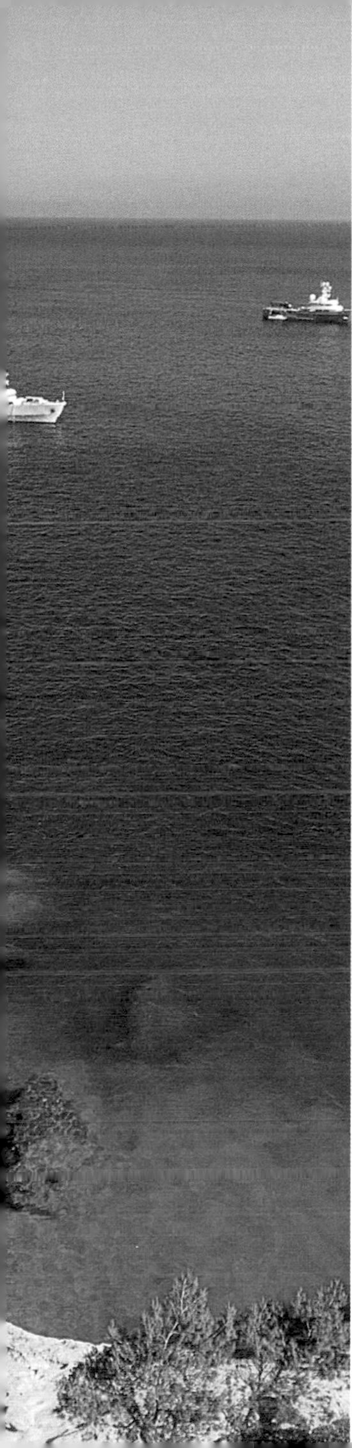

AROUND NAPLES & THE AMALFI COAST

Naples: Spaccanapoli to Capodimonte 68–79

Naples: Toledo to Chaia 80–87

Vesuvius & Around 88–93

The Islands, Sorrento & the South 94–107

Posillipo, Pozzuoli & the North 108–113

Left **Tomb, Sansevero Chapel** Right **Capodimonte**

Spaccanapoli to Capodimonte

THE ANCIENT HEART OF THE CITY IS CELEBRATED *for its striking juxtaposition of chaos and consummate artistry, but most of all for the sheer, boundless energy of the Neapolitan spirit. In many ways, it is an atavistic realm, ruled by its past, including innumerable disasters, but in recent decades a new awareness of its abiding glories has dawned and Old Naples is ready to open anew to the world. Its narrow streets are much safer and cleaner than before and its erstwhile dilapidated, shut-away treasures are now restored and far better organized, without losing any of the uniquely vibrant feeling. Spaccanapoli is the colloquial name for the long, narrow street that runs from Via Duomo to Via Monteoliveto and is the remnant of an ancient Greco-Roman thoroughfare.*

TOP 10 Sights

1. Duomo
2. Museo Archeologico
3. Capodimonte
4. Santa Chiara
5. Sansevero Chapel
6. Piazza Bellini
7. Santi Apostoli
8. Orto Botanico
9. Palazzo dello Spagnolo
10. San Giovanni a Carbonara

Orto Botanico

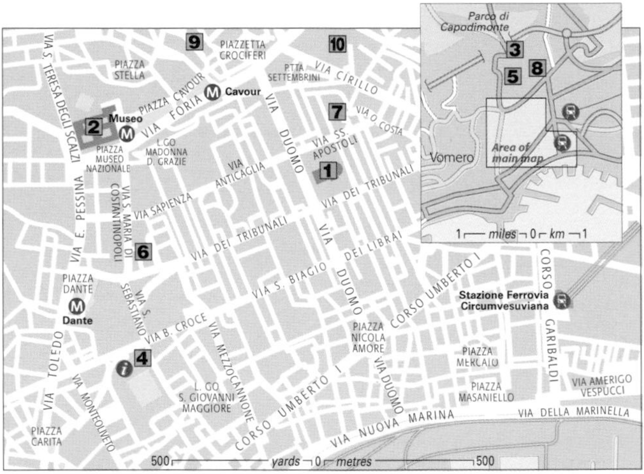

1 Duomo

Although its position in the present-day street-plan seems to be an afterthought and the perfunctory Neo-Gothic façade is less than inspiring, inside Naples' cathedral is a fascinating cornucopia of history, art and local culture. There are ancient remains of the Greek and Roman cities to explore, including some beautiful paleo-Christian mosaics in the baptistry, and splendid art abounds in the main church and its chapels, including the huge work dedicated to the city's patron saint, Gennaro (Januarius) *(see pp12–13)*.

2 Museo Archeologico

One of the world's most important museums of ancient art houses some of the most famous statues from the Greco-Roman past, such as the Callipygean Venus that set standards of physical beauty that have endured through the ages. Other monumental marble works include the Farnese Hercules, but the collections also feature bronzes, mosaics, frescoes, carved semiprecious stone, glassware, Greek vases, Egyptian artifacts, and much more *(see pp14–17)*.

3 Capodimonte

This impressive royal palace is home to important works by some of the greatest masters of all time, including Botticelli, Filippino Lippi, Mantegna, Bellini, Fra' Bartolomeo, Michelangelo, Raphael, Titian, Rembrandt and Dürer, as well as by every great painter working in Naples during the 17th and 18th centuries, including Caravaggio and Ribera *(see pp18–19)*.

4 Santa Chiara

The façade of this structure, rebuilt after World War II, is like a huge cliff of buff-coloured tufa, relieved only by its portico and giant rose window. Only the base of its 14th-century bell-tower is original. Inside the decor has been returned to its Gothic origins, since all the Baroque embellishment was destroyed in wartime bombings. The tomb of Robert of Anjou is the largest funerary monument of medieval Italy, and behind this is the delightful tiled cloister *(see p40)*. *Via Benedetto Croce • Map N3 • Open 8am–12:30pm, 4:30–7:30pm daily (church); 9:30am–1pm, 2:30–5:30pm Mon–Sat, 9:30am–1pm Sun (museum & cloister) • Adm (church free)*

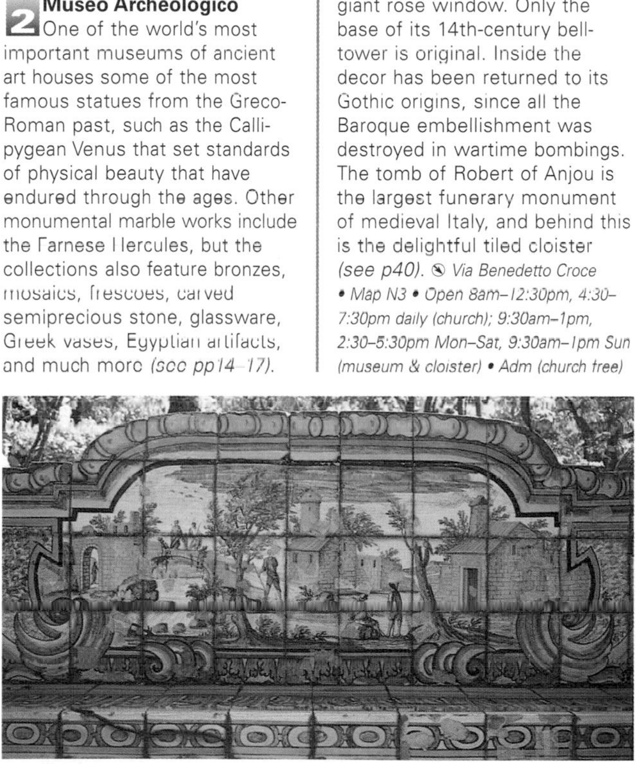

Tiled cloister, Santa Chiara

The Three Guglie

The area's three *guglie* ("needles" or "spires") imitate the original towering contraptions built in the 1600s and 1700s to celebrate feast days. The earliest stone *guglia* was raised to San Gennaro, when the saint supposedly saved Naples from Vesuvius's fury in 1631. Next came one dedicated to San Domenico, as thanks for the end of the plague of 1656. The last adorns Piazza del Gesù, dedicated to the Immaculate Virgin.

5 Sansevero Chapel

Few spaces are decorated with such unity as this family chapel. The credit goes to its designer, the eccentric 18th-century prince Raimondo di Sangro. Full of allegorical symbolism, the statuary are among Naples' most famous, particularly the "veiled" figures of Christ and Modesty. *Via Francesco de Sanctis 19 • Map K1 • Open Nov–Apr: 10am–4:40pm Mon, Wed–Sat, 10am–1pm Sun; May–Oct: 10am–6:40pm Mon, Wed–Sat, 10am–1pm Sun • Adm*

6 Piazza Bellini

This square is one of the most appealing places in Naples, lined with inviting cafés, bookshops and the façades of palaces. Of particular note is the monastery of Sant'Antonio a Port'Alba, incorporating 15th-century Palazzo Conca and adorned with busts of the Spanish royal family. At the centre of the piazza, in addition to a statue of the eponymous composer, is an archaeological excavation, revealing 5th-century BC Greek walls of large tufa blocks *(see p42)*. *Map N2*

Piazza Bellini

7 Santi Apostoli

The original church on this site is believed to have been built in the 5th century over a Roman temple to Mercury. It was rebuilt in the 17th century, with decoration added over the next 100 years. As such it provides a complete treasury of 17th- and 18th-century art, not just by Neapolitan artists but by some the greatest masters of the day. Most famous is the fresco cycle by Lanfranco, with a marvellous *trompe-l'oeil* architectural setting by Codazzi. Other highlights are the altar designed by Borromini and paintings by Giordano in the transept. *Largo Santi Apostoli 9 • Map P1 • Open 8am–1pm, 4:15–8pm Mon–Sat, 9am–1:30pm Sun • Free*

8 Orto Botanico

Created in 1807, this botanical garden remains one of Italy's most important, both in size and in its collections. Given Naples' climate it has been possible to cultivate examples of nearly all of the world's plants and flowers here. Historic structures include the Neo-Classical Serra Temperata, built in 1807 by the same architect who designed the double stairway entrance to the grounds. *Via Floria 223 • Map K1 • 081 44 97 59 • Open 9am–2pm Mon–Fri by appt only • Free*

Staircase, Palazzo dello Spagnolo

9 Palazzo dello Spagnolo

Dating from 1728, this palace offers a fine example of a well-known Neapolitan architectural element, the so-called staircase *"ad ali di falco"* (with falcon wings). Separating two courtyards, the external stairway consists of double flights of steps with tiers of archways, a theatrical feature that became the trademark of its designer, Ferdinando Sanfelice. The palace was owned by a Spanish nobleman, hence the nickname. *Via Vergini 19 • Map P1 • Open 7:30am–2pm, 3:30–8pm Mon–Fri, 7:30am–1pm Sat • Free*

10 San Giovanni a Carbonara

This 14th-century church has no façade of its own but is reached by a double staircase through a courtyard to the left of the Chapel of Santa Monica. Inside are a circular chapel with 15th-century frescoes and bas-reliefs by Spanish masters Bartolomé Ordoñez and Diego de Siloe. *Via Carbonara 5 • Map P1 • Open 9:30am–1pm Mon–Sat • Free*

A Morning at Old Naples' Churches

Begin your tour of Naples' two oldest main streets at Piazza del Gesù, where you can admire the Guglia dell'Immacolata and the rusticated façade of the church. Further along, enter **Santa Chiara** *(see p69)* to take in the medieval tombs and then around the back to see the famous tiled cloister.

Continuing on, stop for a drink at one of the cafés in Piazza San Domenico, where you will note that the Guglia di San Domenico has mermaids sculpted on its base. Across the street, stop in at the church of **Sant'Angelo a Nilo** *(see p74)* to see its Donatello bas-relief, and at the next corner, look for the ancient statue of the god of the Nile, known familiarly as "The Body of Naples". Follow the street all the way to Via Duomo, pausing at the shops of all kinds along the way.

Next, visit the culturally amazing **Duomo** *(see pp12–13)*, and then go behind it to see the earliest *guglia*, topped by a statue of San Gennaro, and Caravaggio's revolutionary painting *The Acts of Mercy* in the **Pio Monte della Misericordia** *(see p41)*. Double back along Via dei Tribunali, where you can visit more fascinating churches, including **San Gregorio Armeno** *(see p74)* and **Santa Maria delle Anime del Purgatorio ad Arco** *(see p74)*.

Finally, head for **Piazza Bellini**, where you can relax and have a drink or a full meal at one of the friendly cafés.

Following pages: **Interior apartment, Capodimonte**

Left **Sant'Angelo a Nilo** Right **San Gregorio Armeno**

TOP 10 Churches

1 Gesù Nuovo

The wall of this church dates back to a 15th-century fortified palace. Inside are works of art from the 16th to 19th centuries. *Piazza del Gesù 2 • Map N3 • Open 7am–12:30pm, 4–7pm Mon–Sat, 7am–2pm, 4–7pm Sun • Free*

2 San Domenico Maggiore

Highlights at this 13th-century church include frescoes by Pietro Cavallini. *Vico S Domenico Maggiore 18 • Map N2 • Open 8:30am–noon, 4:30–7pm daily • Free*

3 Sant'Angelo a Nilo

This 14th-century church houses the *Assumption of the Virgin* by Donatello. *Piazzetta Nilo • Map P3 • Open 10am–noon, 2–4pm Mon–Fri • Free*

4 San Gregorio Armeno

This church is best known for the cult of St Patricia, whose blood "liquefies" each Tuesday. *Via S Gregorio Armeno 1 • Map P2 • Open 9am–noon Mon, Wed–Fri, 9am–12:30pm Sat–Sun • Free*

5 San Lorenzo Maggiore

After World War II bombs reduced much of this church to rubble, it was rebuilt to its 13th-century style, save the Baroque façade. *Via dei Tribunali 316 • Map P2 • Open 8am– noon, 5–7pm daily • Free*

6 San Paolo Maggiore

The 8th-century church still retains two Corinthian columns. *Piazza S Gaetano & Via S Paolo 4 • Map P2 • Open 9am–1:30pm Mon–Sat, 10am–12:30pm Sun • Free*

7 Santa Maria delle Anime del Purgatorio ad Arco

The railings here are adorned with bronze skulls, evoking the tradition of care for the dead. *Via dei Tribunali 39 • Map P2 • Open 9am–1pm Mon–Sat, 9:30am–1pm Sun • Free*

8 San Pietro a Maiella

Built in the 1300s, San Pietro underwent a Baroque makeover in the 1600s then was returned to Gothic style in the 1900s. *Piazza Luigi Miraglia 393 • Map N2 • Open 7:30am–noon, 5:30–7pm Mon–Sat, 8:30am–1pm Sun • Free*

9 Santa Maria di Donnaregina Vecchia

This 13th-century church contains Cavallini frescoes. *Vico Donnaregina 26 • Map P1 • 081 299 101 • Open by appt only • Free*

10 Santa Maria del Carmine

Home to the Madonna Bruna icon, the focus of a Naples cult. *Piazza del Carmine 2 • Map R3 • Open 6:30am–12:30pm, 5–7:30pm Mon–Sat, 6:30am–2pm, 5–7:30pm Sun • Free*

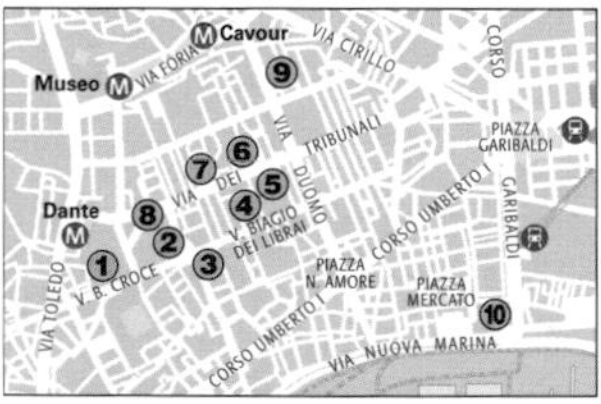

Left **Old print, A.S.** Right **Guitars, Via San Sebastiano**

TOP 10 Traditional Shops

1 A.S.
You never know quite what you'll find in the way of old prints and period objects here – a browse might turn up anything from an 18th-century engraving to an Art Deco-style poster from the 1930s. *Vico Pallonetto a Santa Chiara 38 • Map N3*

2 Affaitati
One of Old Naples' finest antiques shops. Specialities are furniture and ceramics from the 16th to the 19th centuries. Nativity figures are also on offer. *Via B Croce 21 & Via Costantinopoli 18 • Map N3*

3 Napul'é
This little *bottega* (workshop) provides the opportunity to see craftsmen at work, refining the lifelike details of wonderful nativity figures. Most of them are replicas of famous originals, but they will also create personalized versions to order. *Via dei Tribunali 90 • Map P2*

4 Mellinoi
An up-market outlet for stylish clothing, including a good range of designer labels from Italy, France and Spain. *Via B Croce 34 • Map N3*

5 Osmis
This little shop carries a charming line of locally and internationally crafted jewellery, masks, lamps, mirrors and candles. *Via Santa Chiara 10F • Map N3*

6 Tattoo Records
In an appealing little piazza just off Spaccanapoli this funky music shop is good if you're looking for CDs of local music. The proprietor will help you find everything from traditional *tarantella* music to the latest Neapolitan rockers. *Piazzetta Nilo 15 • Map P2*

7 Decumanus
This large store specializes in reproductions of Capodimonte porcelain, as well as other ceramic art from Naples' illustrious past. *Via B Croce 30–31 • Map N3*

8 L'Arte del Pulcinella
This little shop is crammed full of *Pulcinella* figures *(see p46)* in all shapes and sizes, from the sweetly innocent to the bawdy. All in keeping with the character's outlandish personality. *Via dei Tribunali 338 • Map P2*

9 Via San Sebastiano Shops
Along this street, just off Piazza Bellini, you'll find traditional Neapolitan musical instruments, from mandolins to the *triccaballacco* (a three-pronged clacker with cymbals attached). *Map N2*

10 Charcuterie Esposito
Come here for *taralli* (savoury-sweet biscuits), luscious olive oil, local wines and Setaro brand pasta, Naples' best, handmade with basil, porcini mushrooms, lemon or cuttlefish ink. *Via B Croce 43 • Map N3*

Spaccanapoli changes names between Via Toledo and Via del Duomo – from Via Benedetto Croce into Via San Biagio ai Librai.

Left & Right **Intra Moenia**

TOP 10 Old Naples by Night

1 Intra Moenia
This large bar-café-bookshop-publisher is a magnet on this attractive piazza. It's a wonderful place to have a drink and soak up the intellectual ambience. *Piazza Bellini 70 • Map N2*

2 Kinky Bar
This reggae club is not at all kinky – in fact, decidedly mainstream for this city, which seems to love the Caribbean beat. In summer the operation moves outdoors to local beaches. *Via Cisterna dell'Olio 21 • Map N3*

3 Kukuwaya
The tiny dance floor here gets plenty of action to the sounds of funk, reggae or whatever gets people going. Closing time is flexible, tending towards very late. *Via G Paladino 16 • Map P3 • Closed mid-Jul–mid-Sep*

4 Superfly
An excellent, tiny jazz bar, with first-rate drinks and snacks. It's also a sometimes gallery for Naples' new crop of photographers and artists. *Via Cisterna dell'Olio 12 • Map N3 • Closed Jul–Sep*

5 Velvet Zone
The "Velvet" is the top club in the old quarter for dancing, since it stays open until 6am at weekends. Music varies from techno to 1980s to rock, and even to live music from time to time. *Via Cisterna dell'Olio 11 • Map N3 • Closed Mon & Jun–mid-Sep*

6 La Tapas Bar
This relaxed bar occupies the choicest spot on this inviting little piazza. The musical selections tend towards Latin sounds. Despite the name, however, they serve no *tapas*. *Piazzetta del Nilo 36 • Map P2 • Closed Mon–Tue & Aug*

7 Sanakura
This subterranean club is a thriving student hangout – expect a permanent cloud of smoke over the tiny space. Live bands from Italy and around Europe occasionally take to the stage. *Vico Pallonetto a Santa Chiara 5 • Map N3 • Closed Sun–Wed*

8 Lontano da Dove
Come here for an old-fashioned passion for literature – discussions about theatre, art or politics, poetry readings, and, at weekends, live jazz. *Via Bellini 3 • Map N2 • Closed Aug*

9 Bourbon Street
This large jazz club features local talent every evening. In summer the management often organizes jazz cruises around the bay. *Via Bellini 52 • Map N2 • Closed Mon, Jul–Aug*

10 Notting Hill
A long, narrow space with local rock groups, as well as touring Italian and international bands. On Saturdays it becomes "Notting Hill Gallery", a semi-gay club night. *Piazza Dante 88A • Map N2 • Closed Sun–Mon, Jun–Sep*

Left **Gran Caffè Aragonese** Right **Gelateria della Scimmia**

TOP 10 Cafés, Gelaterie & Pasticcerie

1 Gran Caffè Aragonese
This café dominates the scene on this beautiful and crowded piazza. It offers a good range of local desserts and savoury snacks, and excellent Neapolitan-style coffee. *Piazza S Domenico Maggiore 5–8 • Map N2*

2 Scaturchio
Noted all over Naples for its wonderful traditional pastries, it's a real treat to sample the wares while checking out this piazza. Don't arrive too late or you may find they've sold out. *Piazza S Domenico Maggiore 19 • Map N2*

3 Bar Mexico
This café is reputed to have the best *espresso* in town, but if you don't want it sweetened *(alla napoletana)* then ask for a *caffè amaro* (bitter coffee). A hot-weather winner is the *frappe di caffè* (iced whipped coffee). You can also stock up on some wonderful coffee blends to take home. *Piazza Dante 86 • Map N2*

4 Caffè dell'Epoca
Dating back to 1886, this place knows all about quality. Enjoy an *espresso* and a *cornetto* (croissant) at one of the outside tables – or make like a local and stand at the bar. *Via Sta Maria di Costantinopoli 82 • Map N2*

5 Gelateria della Scimmia
This is one of the city's oldest and most famous *gelaterie* (ice-cream parlours) so expect a crowd. *Piazza Carità 4 • Map N3*

6 Berevino
The perfect wine bar to sample an extensive array of Campanian wines, as well as some fine national selections. *Via S Sebastiano 62 • Map N3*

7 Chocolat
This attractive little place features 30 different kinds of chocolate, *granite* (chunky sorbets) and many varieties of *cappuccino*. A great atmosphere. *Via S Pietro a Maiella 8 • Map N2*

8 Intra Moenia
The mainstay of Piazza Bellini and a good place to hang out and enjoy a drink. In warm weather it's also a lively gay venue in the evenings *(see p76)*.

9 Caffè Arabo
Not just a great café with an appealing atmosphere, but a purveyor of delicious Arabic goodies and full meals *(see p79)*.

10 Internetbar
This trendy establishment offers Internet facilities, drinks and snacks, and an art gallery. *Piazza Bellini 74 • Map N2*

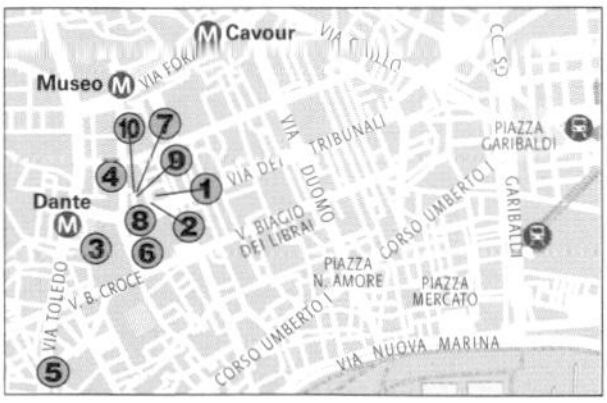

Left **L'Antica Pizzeria "da Michele"** Right **La Trianon da Ciro**

Top 10 Pizzerie

1 L'Antica Pizzeria "da Michele"

The most traditional of Naples' *pizzerie*, the menu here is limited to only two classic varieties, *margherita* and *marinara*. Still, the taste is sublime – and the wait often considerable. Take a number at the door before queueing. *Via Cesare Sersale 1–3 • Map Q2 • 081 553 92 04 • No credit cards • €*

2 La Trianon da Ciro

Equally traditional as "da Michele" – and just across the street – this eatery is more upmarket, with a larger choice. The decor is appealing, recalling the city's *belle époque* heyday. *Via Pietro Colletta 42–6 • Map Q2 • 081 553 94 26 • No credit cards • €*

3 Lombardi a Santa Chiara

A treat from the beginning of the meal to the end – good pizza, wine and fine *dolci* (desserts). *Via B Croce 59 • Map N3 • 081 552 07 80 • €*

4 Di Matteo

As well as pizza, try some *frittura* here – deep-fried titbits of vegetables, rice and cheese. *Via dei Tribunali 94 • Map P2 • 081 45 52 62 • No credit cards • €*

5 Il Pizzaiolo del Presidente

Another *pizzeria* on this busy street, which gained its moment of fame when then US President Bill Clinton stopped by for a snack. *Via dei Tribunali 120–1 • Map P2 • 081 21 09 03 • No credit cards • €*

6 Friggitoria-Pizzeria Giuliano

A good place to head for *pizzetta* (mini-pizza). A little fresh tomato, cheese and basil is all it takes to send this into the firmament of Neapolitan culinary heaven. *Calata Trinità Maggiore 33 • Map N3 • 081 551 09 86 • No credit cards • €*

7 I Re di Napoli

One of a chain of three, the choice of pizzas here is wider than in the more stalwart places. Try the one with mini mozzarella balls. *Piazza Dante 16 • Map N2 • 081 544 72 30 • €*

8 Pizzeria Sorbillo

The main restaurant dates from 1935 but there is also a stand-up branch next door that is even more fun because you can watch them twirl the dough, dash on the topping and pop it into the brick oven. *Via dei Tribunali 35 • Map N2 • No credit cards • €*

9 Pizzeria Vesi

This place specializes in "pizza DOC" – an aromatic combination of mozzarella balls, *pomodorini* (cherry tomatoes) and basil. *Via dei Tribunali 388 • Map P2 • 081 29 99 95 • No credit cards • €*

10 Pizzeria Fortuna

Little more than a counter with a few plastic tables in front, this little place turns out delicious *pizzette* and other goodies in seconds. *Via PS Mancini 8 • Map R2 • 081 20 53 80 • No credit cards • €*

At the best pizza restaurants in Naples you will see a certificate of authentication hanging outside the premises.

Above **La Cantina del Sole**

Price Categories

For a three-course meal for one with half a bottle of wine (or equivalent meal), taxes and extra charges.	€	under €20
	€€	€20–€30
	€€€	€30–€40
	€€€€	€40–€50
	€€€€€	over €50

Top 10 Restaurants

1 Mimì alla Ferrovia

Mimì specializes in fish and seafood, but they also have great *pasta e ceci* (pasta soup with chickpeas). *Via Alfonso d'Aragona 19 • Map R1 • 081 553 85 25 • Closed Sun, 2 weeks Aug • €€€*

2 Cantina della Sapienza

The menu changes daily but is always authentic. Dishes such as *melanzane alla parmigiana* (aubergine/eggplant with mozzarella and tomato). *Via della Sapienza 40 • Map N2 • 081 45 90 78 • Closed D, Sun, Aug • No credit cards • €*

3 La Cantina del Sole

Noted for recipes that hark back as far as the 1600s, choices are impressive. *Via G Paladino 3 • Map P3 • 081 552 73 12 • Closed Mon, Tue–Sat L, Aug • €€€*

4 Bellini

This *trattoria* specializes in seafood pasta and grilled catch of the day. *Via Sta Maria di Costantinopoli 79–80 • Map N2 • 081 45 97 74 • Closed Sun, 1 wk Aug • €€*

5 Simposium

The table is communal, waiters are in period costume, and the entertainment and food are based on historic eras. Book ahead. *Via B Croce 38 • Map N3 • 081 551 85 10 • Closed Mon–Thu, Fri & Sun L • €€*

6 La Vecchia Cantina

Taking full advantage of its location next to the market, this place serves seriously fresh fish at delightful prices. *Vico S Nicola alla Carità 13–14 • Map M3 • 081 552 02 26 • Closed Tue & Sun D, 2 wks Aug • €*

7 Capasso

An economical choice near the major central sights. Delicious pizza. *Via Porta S Gennaro 2-3 • Map P1 • 081 45 64 21 • Closed Tue • No credit cards • €*

8 Caffè Arabo

This establishment turns out full Middle Eastern meals. The kebabs are perfectly grilled and the honeyed desserts superb. *Piazza Bellini 64 • Map N2 • 081 442 06 07 • No credit cards • €*

9 Lombardi

A restaurant and a *pizzeria* that is a bit off the beaten track, so rarely crowded. The *antipasto* buffet is wonderful, featuring seasonal delicacies. *Via Foria 12 • Map P1 • 081 45 62 20 • Closed Mon • €€*

10 Un Sorriso Integrale

Naples' only specialized vegetarian restaurant. The menu might include black-eyed peas with greens or risotto with artichokes. *Via S Pietro a Maiella 6 • Map N2 • 081 45 50 26 • No credit cards • €*

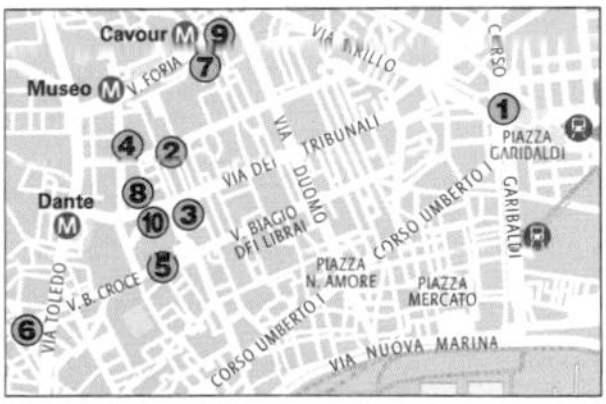

Note: Unless otherwise stated, all restaurants accept credit cards and serve vegetarian meals

Left **Palazzo Reale** Right **Castel Sant'Elmo**

Naples: Toledo to Chiaia

THE FIRST IMPRESSION OF THE AREA KNOWN AS "ROYAL NAPLES" *is of spaciousness and light. This is Naples' showcase: a vision of how functional the city can be with due appreciation for its setting. Elegant architecture from various ages graces the terrain here, which is also home to one of the most authentic neighbourhoods, maritime Santa Lucia. Above it all, the Vomero district boasts a fine castle and monastery overlooking the bay and one of the city's best parks, while to the west is the lively Mergellina district, with its working port and busy restaurants lined up along the coast.*

Galleria Umberto I

Top 10 Sights

1. Palazzo Reale
2. Castel Nuovo
3. Certosa di San Martino
4. San Francesco di Paola
5. Teatro San Carlo
6. Galleria Umberto I
7. Castel dell'Ovo
8. Villa Comunale
9. Museo Nazionale della Ceramica Duca di Martina
10. Castel Sant'Elmo

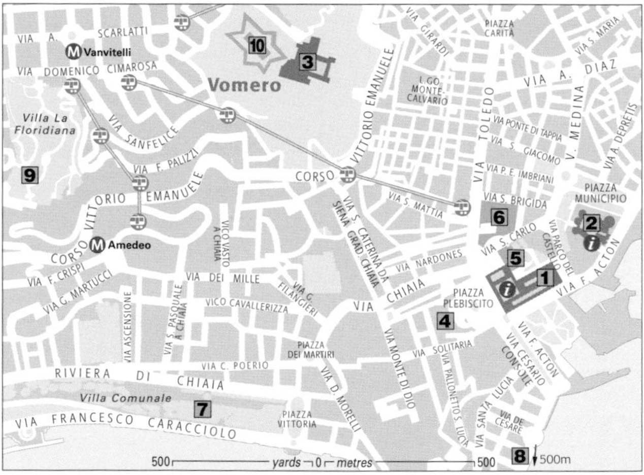

1 Palazzo Reale

The Royal Palace is largely 18th-century in character, with its vast layout, imposing façade and important rooms such as the ballroom and the chapel. However, later embellishments took a Neo-Classical turn, in particular the marvellous grand staircase. Under Napoleonic rule many of the rooms received a thorough makeover, which dominates the decor today. Don't miss the fine Renaissance and Baroque paintings from the royal collection, including works by Guercino, Spadarino and several Flemish masters *(see pp8–9)*.

2 Castel Nuovo

This rather sombre fortress is a study in stylistic contrasts – in direct opposition to its bulky grey towers, the marble Triumphal Arch exudes the delicacy of the early Renaissance. Inside, the spartan blankness is relieved by the wondrously complex ceiling of the Barons' Hall, while the fresco fragments and sculptures in the chapel juxtapose with the harsh reality of the dungeons. In addition there are fine collections of religious and secular artwork. Go up to the battlements to take in the panorama *(see pp10–11)*.

3 Certosa di San Martino

If there is one place that could be called the true museum of Naples, this is it. So varied are the collections and the architecture that all aspects of the city's history and cultural output seem to be represented here. These include a large collection of Nativity scenes and figures, some of Naples' most significant paintings and sculptures, views of the city painted in different eras, a decorative arts collection, and the exuberantly Baroque church, decorated by the best Neapolitan artists of the 17th and 18th centuries *(see pp20–23)*.

4 San Francesco di Paola

The impetus to build this imitation Pantheon came from the Napoleonic king Joachim Murat (1808–15). Completed under the reinstated Bourbon dynasty, the idea was to do away with the chaotic jumble around the palace by recreating a version of the ancient Roman temple to the gods and setting it off with arcades echoing those of St Peter's. It dominates a semicircular piazza with the Palazzo Reale at the opposite end *(see p40)*. *Piazza del Plebiscito • Map M6 • Open 8am–noon, 3:30–6pm Mon–Sat, 8am–1pm Sun • Free*

San Francesco di Paola

The Birth of Grand Opera

Along with its many other musical accomplishments, Italy is the home of opera. Inspired by Classical Greek drama, the first opera was composed by northerner Monteverdi towards the end of the 16th century. But it was Naples, renowned for its inimitable *castrati* *(see p47)*, who really made the genre its own. The accompanying sets, costumes and dance were refined, and the whole artform soon went international.

5 Teatro San Carlo

Actually an appendage to the Palazzo Reale, built by order of King Charles, this opera house predates the famous La Scala in Milan by some 40 years. Officially opened on 4 November 1737, it has never ceased to be one of the most important and innovative opera houses in the world. The interior was originally done up in the Bourbon colours of silver, gold and sky blue, but after being rebuilt following a fire in 1816 the colour scheme is now mostly gold and red, though no less sumptuous. It was compared by French writer Stendhal to an Oriental emperor's palace. *Via San Carlo 98F • Map N5 • Open for guided tours 10am–7pm daily • Adm*

6 Galleria Umberto I

Part of the Urban Renewal Plan following the cholera epidemic of 1884 *(see p37)*, this light-filled space is home to elegant buildings with Neo-Renaissance embellishments and marble floors, overarched by a roof of iron and glass. Located across from the Royal Palace and Teatro San Carlo, the spot immediately became popular with the city's smart and artistic set, and even today has an air of bygone charm. *Piazza Trieste e Trento to Via Toledo • Map N5*

7 Castel dell'Ovo

In ancient times, this spot was part of the vast estate of the Roman general Lucullus. At the end of the 5th century an order of monks founded a monastery here, then the Normans built the first castle. It was modified by succeeding dynasties, achieving its present form in the 16th century. Legend has it that its name derives from a magic egg *(uovo)* hidden inside, supposedly placed there by the Roman poet Virgil. The building is now used for cultural events. *Via Partenope • Map K2 • Open 9am–6pm Mon–Sat, 9am–1:30pm Sun • Free*

Teatro San Carlo

8 Villa Comunale

Designed by Luigi Vanvitelli and inaugurated in 1781 as the royal gardens, this large, public park, lying right on the bay, was completely refurbished in 1994. It is graced with many 19th-century copies of Classical statuary, and was once home to the monumental ancient work, the Farnese Bull

To book tickets for the Teatro San Carlo, and for more information on its current productions, visit www.teatrosancarlo.it

Villa Comunale

group, now in the Museo Archeologico *(see p16)*. Other adornments include a Neo-Classical aquarium, Europe's oldest, and a magnificent iron and glass bandstand *(see p43)*. ✆ *Via Caracciolo • Map K6 • Open May–Oct: 7am–midnight daily; Nov–Apr: 7am–10pm daily*

9 Museo Nazionale della Ceramica Duca di Martina

Since 1927 this former villa of a king's morganatic wife has been home to a prestigious collection of European and Oriental decorative art. Of the 6,000 objects, highlights are Hispano-Moorish lustreware, Italian majolica tiles, Limoges porcelain and 18th-century Oriental porcelain *(see p39)*. ✆ *Villa Floridiana, Via Cimarosa 77 • Map J5 • Open for guided tours: 9:30am, 11am, 12:30pm Tue–Sun • Adm*

10 Castel Sant'Elmo

This Angevin castle dating from 1329 was upgraded to its six-point configuration in the 16th century, giving it a militaristic presence looming above the city. In later centuries it was used as a prison, remaining in military possession until 1976. It now houses libraries and cultural activities. ✆ *Via Tito Angelini 22 • Map L4 • Open 9am–7pm Tue–Sun • Adm*

A Day in Royal Naples

Morning

Begin your tour inside **Galleria Umberto I**, where you can enjoy a morning *cappuccino* at Caffè Roma *(No. 25–6)* and get a sense of the bustling optimism of 19th-century Naples. Coming out onto Via San Carlo, the elegant Neo-Classical façade of the **Teatro San Carlo** is directly across the street.

Go to the right and around the corner into Piazza del Plebiscito. On your right is the massive dome of the church of **San Francesco di Paola** *(see p81)*, and on your left, **Palazzo Reale** *(see pp8–9)*. First walk over to the church, noting the bronze equestrian statues of kings Charles III and Ferdinand I, then go back across the piazza to the Royal Palace. Enter the courtyard and take the magnificent staircase up to the apartments.

Take a break for a snack or lunch at historic **Gambrinus** *(see p87)*, just outside the piazza.

Afternoon

After lunch go back past the Teatro San Carlo and the palace gardens, and be sure not to miss the giant statues of the horse-tamers at the gate. Continue on down and across the lawns to the **Castel Nuovo** *(see pp10–11)*. Your visit here should include the views from the parapets.

Finally, head up Via Medina to the **Caffetteria Medina** *(see p87)*, where you can enjoy a drink while admiring the Fountain of Neptune.

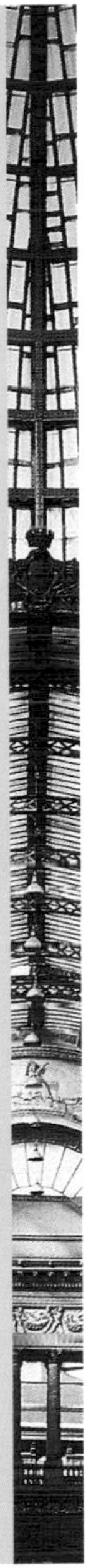

Don't follow the Royal Naples itinerary on Sundays, when the Palazzo Reale is closed.

Above **Teatro Bellini façade**

TOP 10 Performing Arts Venues

1 Associazione Scarlatti
This is the best of Naples' small musical companies, offering classical chamber music and the occasional jazz group. A typical evening might feature the music of Debussy, Ravel, Chausson and Franck. *Teatro delle Palme, Vico Vetriera 12 • Map L5*

2 Augusteo
Musical comedies are a speciality at this theatre, which is also one of the few that may offer shows outside the usual season of October to May. A chance to see what contemporary productions are like, in line with the centuries-old tradition of excellent comic theatre in Naples. *Piazzetta Augusteo • Map L5*

3 Bellini
Mainstream theatre and touring international musicals (usually in English) are featured here, as well as dance, local musicals and concerts. Recent international productions have included Prokofiev's *Romeo and Juliet* and *Fiddler on the Roof*. *Via Conte di Ruvo 14-19 • Map N2*

4 Galleria Toledo
This small modern theatre, in the thick of the teeming Quartieri Spagnoli, offers more challenging theatrical fare, both intelligent, avant-garde local works and new international fringe and experimental plays, translated into Italian. *Via Concezione a Montecalvario 36 • Map M4*

5 Mercadante
Opened in 1779, this historic theatre hosts productions touring Italy, some of them quite off-beat. *Piazza Municipio 1 • Map N5*

6 Politeama
This large, modern space offers international music, dance and drama. Recent international performers have included German cutting-edge dancer Pina Bausch and US composer Philip Glass. *Via Monte di Dio 80 • Map M6*

7 Sancarluccio
Small companies gravitate here, alternating with cabaret shows. Everything from Shakespeare to Existentialism. *Via S Pasquale a Chiaia 49 • Map K6*

8 Teatro Nuovo
Fringe, experimental and the best of new international theatre is the keynote here. *Via Concezione a Montecalvario 16 • Map M4*

9 Bracco
Lively local productions, often in dialect. A typical season might include titles such as *Una moglie coi baffi* (A Moustachioed Wife) or *Le sorprese del divorzio* (The Surprises of Divorce). *Via Tarsia 40 • Map M2*

10 Sannazaro
This lovely theatre dates from 1874 and features its own company, often performing works in Neapolitan dialect. *Via Chiaia 157 • Map M5*

For details of current productions at Naples' theatres visit the website www.agendaonline.it

Left **Antiques** Right **Murano glass**

TOP 10 Shopping

1 Bowinkel
One of Naples' finest dealers in old books and prints. Expect to find Italian prints that are centuries-old as well as more modern ones, and a host of other Neapolitan memorabilia. *Piazza dei Martiri 24 • Map L6*

2 Maison d'Art
One of the best antiques shops in the city, it's rather like browsing through a museum. Real treasures are on display, including 19th-century gouaches of Neapolitan panoramas, 17th-century ceramics and 16th-century bronze candlesticks. Prices are high. *Via Sta Teresa a Chiaia 18 • Map K5*

3 Penna & Carta 1989
Come to this pleasant shop for art supplies, fine handmade stationery and top-quality fountain pens, including decorative hand-blown glass pens. *Largo Vasto a Chiaia 86 • Map K5*

4 La Murrina
These elegant rooms are filled with fine Murano glass, in all shapes, sizes and colours. Exquisite vases, bowls and paperweights. *Via S Carlo 18 • Map N5*

5 Fusaro
This local chain specializes in designer gear for men – shoes, suits, shirts and ties, jeans and jackets, as well as caps, bags and belts. *Via Chiaia 33 & Via Toledo 276 • Map M5*

6 Maffei
Stylish jewellery at affordable prices. Silver and gold are featured, with an emphasis on modern pieces compatible with today's taste. Some original lines by local artisans are featured. *Via Sta Teresa a Chiaia 10–11 • Map K5*

7 Fratelli Tramontano
Italians are known the world over for their leather goods, including bags and shoes. Traditional Neapolitan craftsmanship is the byword here. *Via Chiaia 142–3 • Map M5*

8 Rino Corcione
One of several coral and cameo shops on and near this beautiful piazza. This one boasts a vast selection of pieces, some at highly affordable prices. *Piazzale S Martino 14-11 • Map L3*

9 La Bottega della Ceramica
The south of Italy is known for its hand-painted ceramics. A host of traditional designs are featured here, from simple earthenware beakers to decorative plates with complex scenes. *Via Carlo Poerio 40 • Map L6*

10 Dolce & Amaro
Thirty-five types of chocolate await you here. Treats include *limoncello*-flavoured dark chocolate and chocolate Neapolitan landmarks, such as Vesuvius. Or how about an all-chocolate coffee-maker with all-chocolate cups? *Via Chiaia 123 • Map M5*

Left **Aret' a' Palm** Right **S'move**

Top 10 Nightlife

1 Baracdero
This bar captures the charm of the Santa Lucia quarter, immortalized in one of the most famous Neapolitan songs. By the water, near Castel dell'Ovo, it's great for hanging out and enjoying the views. *Banchina Sta Lucia 2 • Map N6*

2 Aret' a' Palm
The name is Neapolitan for "behind the palm", which is just where this bar is located, on a laid-back piazza. Crowds show up at this stylish spot for the mix of world music and jazzy sounds. *Piazza Sta Maria La Nova 14 • Map N3 • Closed Mon–Fri*

3 Vibes
This bustling bar features live music late into the night at weekends. It's also a café and a restaurant, with a tiny, inviting interior and seating outside in the square. *Largo S Giovanni Maggiore 26–7 • Map P3*

4 Ex-ess
One of the ritziest clubs in town. The music tends towards house and other sophisticated electronic sounds. *Via G Martucci 28–30 • Map K5 • Closed Jun–Sep*

5 S'move
Another chic venue, but less pretentious. Although there's no dance floor, the good selection of music keeps things moving. *Vico dei Sospiri 10A • Map L6 • Closed Aug*

6 Otto Jazz
A Neapolitan tradition for jazz enthusiasts, this club spotlights local musicians and more mainstream trends in jazz, with a dash of southern Italian folk music. *Salita Cariati 23 • Map M5 • Closed Jul*

7 Around Midnight
This live jazz venue focuses on standards and classics most of the time, booking local performers from around Italy. *Via G Bonito 32A • Map K3*

8 Contatto
Attracting mostly 20-somethings, Thursday is gay night at this disco-pub, with a country & western theme. In summer, the terrace is a nice plus, although the location is rather out of the way. *Antica Birreria Edenlandia: Via Oderico da Pordenone, off Via Kennedy • Map J2*

9 Virgilio Club
This semi-gay venue is quite serenely sophisticated, taking full advantage of the pine-scented setting on summer nights. *Via Tito Lucrezio Caro 6 • Map J2*

10 Freezer
This ultra-modern discobar, northeast of Piazza Garibaldi, turns over-the-top gay once a week. It seems to attract every one of the city's diverse gay residents, out for a good time. *Via Lauria 6, Centro Direzionale, Isola G6 • Map K1 • Closed Aug*

Above **Caffè Gambrinus**

Price Categories

For a three-course meal for one with half a bottle of wine (or equivalent meal), taxes and extra charges.

€	under €20
€€	€20–€30
€€€	€30–€40
€€€€	€40–€50
€€€€€	over €50

TOP 10 Places to Eat

1 Caffè Gambrinus
This *belle époque* institution still retains much of its original decor. It was popular with free-thinking intellectuals and writers in the past and closed down by the Fascists as a result. The pastries and buffet lunch are particularly good. *Via Chiaia 1–2 • Map M5 • €*

2 Caffetteria Medina
The café's main claim to fame is its location right next to the Neptune Fountain. Tables outside provide you with an excellent vantage point. *Via Medina 30–31 • Map P4 • €*

3 Pintauro
This traditional *pasticceria* (pastry shop) is an excellent choice for procuring the signature Neapolitan sweets, particularly *sfogliatella* and *babà* *(see p61)*. *Via Toledo 275 • Map N4 • €*

4 Pinterré
This seaside café is a great place for kicking back and watching the world go by, with some of the city's most captivating views. Excellent snacks, as well. *Via Partenope 12 • Map K2 • €*

5 Brandi
A Naples institution, laying claim to having invented the pizza margherita on the occasion of a visit from Italy's Queen Margherita in 1889. There's also a full restaurant menu. *Salita Sant'Anna di Palazzo 1 • Map M5 • €€€*

6 I Re di Napoli
This *pizzeria* chain serves traditional pizzas with a range of topping choices. *Piazza Trieste e Trento 7–8 • Map M5 • 081 42 30 13 • €*

7 La Stanza del Gusto
Hidden away at the top of a flight of stairs just off Via Chiaia, this is gourmet dining, with dishes crafted according to seasonal choices. *Vicoletto Sant'Arpino 21 • Map M5 • 081 40 15 78 • Closed Sun–Mon • €€€*

8 'a Taverna 'e zi Carmela
This tucked-away family-run establishment has lots of charm. The speciality is seafood. *Via Niccolò Tommaseo 11–12 • Map L6 • Closed Sun • €€*

9 Osteria da Tonino
Excellent dishes here include seafood stew. Always lively. *Via Sta Teresa a Chiaia 47 • Map K5 • 081 42 15 33 • Closed Sun, Aug • €€*

10 Lo Chalet
Excellent seafood and pasta combinations. *Via F Caracciolo, by Largo Sermoneta, Mergellina • Map K2 • 081 68 17 05 • €€*

***Note:** Unless otherwise stated, all restaurants accept credit cards and serve vegetarian meals*

Left **Herculaneum** Right **Hiking Mount Vesuvius**

Vesuvius and Around

FEW PLACES ON EARTH ARE AS AWE-INSPIRING AS THIS AREA *of southern Italy. Here lies the archetypal heart of Campania, where high culture and the indifferent violence of Nature have met again and again. Although men and women lost their families, homes and lives, mankind has ironically gained from these deadly encounters with the mighty volcano that is Mount Vesuvius – in the very act of destruction entire cultures have been miraculously preserved for posterity. Here can be found the ancient city of Pompeii, the town of Herculaneum, and other amazing villas – all of them replete with timeless art and architecture that uniquely reveals to us the great heritage of beauty bequeathed to us by our forebears from Roman times. In later centuries, the unearthing of these treasures inspired even kings to build sumptuous palaces nearby, so that they could experience firsthand the exciting discoveries, although some are now sadly in decay.*

Roman forum, Pompeii

Top 10 Sights

1. Pompeii
2. Herculaneum
3. Torre Annunziata & Oplontis
4. Castellamare di Stabia
5. Vesuvius
6. Reggia di Portici & the Vesuvian Villas
7. Villa Campolieto
8. Villa Favorita
9. Villa Ruggiero
10. Torre del Greco

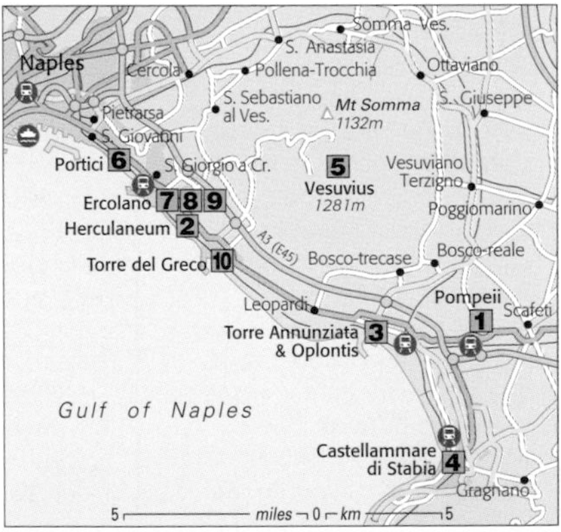

Note that the modern town of Pompei is spelt with only one "i".

1 Pompeii

Certainly no archaeological find is more important than that of ancient Pompeii, where a culture was captured forever by the eruption of Mount Vesuvius in AD 79. Not only can we see the streets, buildings, furnishings, art, tools, jewellery, and even the food and drink of the people who lived here, but plaster casts reveal the people themselves. From the ruling class down to slaves, we can see their last moments during those terrible few hours that doomed the city *(see pp24–5)*.

2 Herculaneum

This town, largely a resort in ancient times located right on the sea, was also buried alive by by mud and lava from Vesuvius. The resulting preservation is, if anything, even better, bringing down to us wooden structures and other more perishable materials. However the excavations began in the 18th century when the science of archaeology had yet to be developed, so diggers were not very careful, being mostly on a royal treasure hunt for statuary, mosaics and fresco paintings *(see pp26–7)*

3 Torre Annunziata & Oplontis

Few places present such a stark contrast to the visitor as this one. The contemporary squalor of uncontrolled urban blight hides, within its depressed grime, imperial splendours of the ancient world. The town is infamous these days for its crime and poverty, yet just two blocks from the train station lie the beautifully preserved ruins of one of the most sumptuous villas to have been preserved by Vesuvius's eruption *(see pp26–7)*.

Promenade, Castellammare di Stabia

4 Castellammare di Stabia

This port town has been known since ancient times for its thermal springs – the many different waters are each thought to be therapeutic in specific ways. As with its neighbours, its beauty has been compromised by poverty and developers in recent decades, but it is not without charm, particularly along the central promenade. Nearby, the ruins of aristocratic villas, Arianna and San Marco, offer glimpses into wealthy lifestyles of 2,000 years ago *(see pp26–7)*.

5 Vesuvius

Continental Europe's only active volcano has not blown up since its last rumble in 1944, but experts say it could happen at any time. Yet a relatively easy walk to the crater is certainly a memorable experience. Either drive or take a bus or train to Ercolano-Scavi station, from where the 1.5-hour return trail is accompanied by volcanologist guides, except in bad weather *(see p25)*. *Map D3 • Guided walks 9am–5pm daily • Adm*

Following pages: **Pompeii flanked by Mount Vesuvius**

The Golden Mile

The 18th-century evolution of *Il Miglio d'Oro* can be traced back to Maria Amalia Cristina, Queen of Naples. She had grown up in a Viennese palace adorned with two marble statues unearthed at Herculaneum. When she arrived in Naples, she wanted a palace near the site. It started a trend among the nobility and in the end some 120 villas were built.

6 Reggia di Portici & the Vesuvian Villas

The Vesuvian Villas were begun by King Charles III and Queen Maria in the 18th century. His *Reggia* (palace), designed by Antonio Medrano, was the first and greatest of the villas, the rest of which were built by other members of the Bourbon court. For the most part the villas are now dilapidated, but there are plans to save as many as possible. *Reggia di Portici, Via Università 100 • Map L2 • Open Sep–Jul: 8:30am–7pm Mon–Fri • Free*

7 Villa Campolieto

This stupendous villa was designed by the Vanvittelli brothers between 1760–75. It features a circular portico, where concerts are now held, and enjoys a lovely panorama of the bay. Some of the rooms have been restored to their original decor, while others are used for special exhibitions. *Corso Resina 283, Ercolano • Map L2 • Open 10am–1pm Tue–Sun • Free*

8 Villa Favorita

Villa Favorita was boarded up at least 100 years ago – with Italian Unification the noble homes became an obsolete symbol of decadence. However the park and the annexe are open to visitors, the former punctuated with pavilions. *Corso Resina 291, Ercolano • Map L2 • Open 10am–1pm Tue–Sun • Free*

9 Villa Ruggiero

Set further back from the sea, this house was built for the baronial Petti family. It has now been fully restored, with Rococo decorations, frescoes and marble busts. *Via A Rossi 40, Ercolano • Map L2 • Open 10am–1pm Tue–Sun • Free*

10 Torre del Greco

This town has been home to coral artisans and cameo manufacturers for centuries, a craft that continues to draw admirers today. Yet its rough streets are among the area's worst for violent crime and, to add to the tension, it lies in the direct line of fire from Vesuvius, last suffering destruction in 1794. *Map L2*

Torre del Greco

The Museo del Corallo in Torre del Greco exhibits the local coral craft (Piazza Luigi Palomba 6 • Open 9am–noon Mon–Fri • Free).

Price Categories		
For a three-course meal for one with half a bottle of wine (or equivalent meal), taxes and extra charges.	€	under €20
	€€	€20–€30
	€€€	€30–€40
	€€€€	€40–€50
	€€€€€	over €50

Above **Seafood dish, Al Gamberone**

Top 10 Places to Eat

1 Il Principe, Pompei

The elegant decor is graced with reproductions of Pompeian art, and the cuisine, too, takes its inspiration from ancient sources. Classical writers and the remains of the city have both provided recipes, which have been adapted to modern tastes. The food has earned the proprietors a Michelin star. *Piazza B Longo 8 • Map E4 • 081 850 55 66 • Closed Sun, Mon D & Nov–Mar • €€€€€*

2 Internazionale Restaurant, Cafeteria & Bar, Pompeii

Located inside the archaeological site, near the Forum Baths, this place offers bar service, a self-service cafeteria and a restaurant, with seating under the colonnade. The food is not bad, but the biggest plus is a break from the intensive sightseeing. *Map E4 • 081 861 07 77 • No credit cards • €€*

3 Ristorante Suisse, Pompeii

Of all the eateries outside the main gate of the ruins this one offers the nicest atmosphere, with indoor and outside tables. Standard *trattoria* fare. *Piazza Porta Marina Inferiore • Map E4 • 081 861 01 85 • €€*

4 Zi Caterina, Pompei

Seafood is a speciality here; try *seppie con finocchi e olive* (cuttlefish with fennel and olives). The wine list features local vintages. *Via Roma 20 • Map E4 • 081 850 26 07 • Closed Tue D • €€*

5 Al Gamberone, Pompei

Seafood is the keynote here, in particular giant prawns *(gamberone)*. Dining *al fresco* under the lemon and orange trees is a treat. *Via Piave 36 • Map E4 • 081 850 68 14 • Closed Fri • €€*

6 Nuovo Ristorante Anfiteatro, Pompei

Located immediately outside the excavations. Try the succulent *baccalà* (salt cod). *Via Plinio 9 • Map E4 • 081 850 60 42 • Closed Fri • €€*

7 Bar degli Amorini, Ercolano

Enjoy a simple meal and the chilled red wine, made on the premises. *Corso Resina • Map L2 • No phone • No credit cards • €*

8 Calcagno, Ercolano

This modest *trattoria* serves pasta, risotto and grilled fish. *Corso Italia 17, Ercolano • Map L2 • 081 739 04 05 • Closed Sun • €*

9 La Mammola, Torre del Greco

A beautifully decorated restaurant which serves traditional cuisine with creative flair. *Hotel Marad, Via S Sebastiano 24 • Map L2 • 081 849 21 68 • €€€*

10 Grand Hotel La Medusa, Castellammare di Stabia

This elegant hotel has a large dining room offering set meals, as well as *à la carte* selections. *Via Passeggiata Archeologica 5 • Map E4 • 081 872 33 83 • €€*

***Note:** Unless otherwise stated, all restaurants accept credit cards and serve vegetarian meals*

Left **Beach, Capri** Right **Ischia port**

The Islands, Sorrento and the South

THIS IS ONE OF THE WORLD'S MOST INTENSELY EMOTIVE ZONES, *where verdant-crowned cliffs plunge into the royal-blue sea. This is where the Homeric hero Ulysses went astray on his homeward voyage, daring to listen to the fateful song of the Sirens while his stalwart men, their ears plugged with wax, continued onward, away from charmed death. On these islands is where the Greeks first brought their high culture to the area, where Roman emperors lived in stupendous luxury, and where, in more recent times, the world's most glamorous celebrities indulged in their own lavish lifestyles. When the American writer John Steinbeck first saw the Amalfi Coast he was moved to uncontrollable weeping. He was not the first – nor will he be the last – to succumb to the emotional impact of the potent beauty found here.*

Top 10 Sights

1. Capri
2. Ravello
3. Paestum
4. Ischia
5. Procida
6. Vico Equense
7. Sorrento
8. Massa Lubrense
9. The Amalfi Coast
10. Salerno

Temple, Paestum

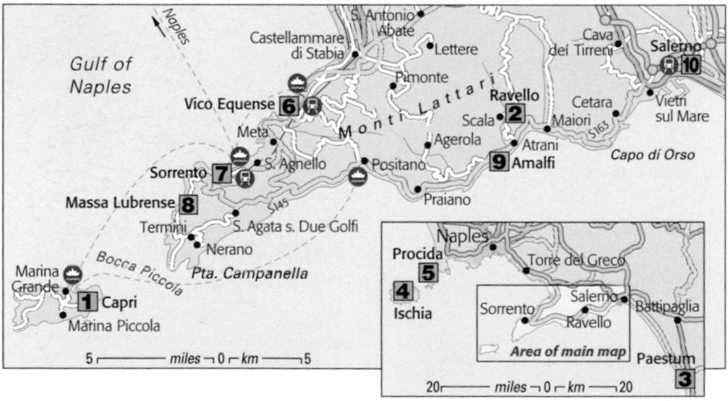

1 Capri

The fabled isle has had its detractors – it has been called "nothing more than a rocky cliff with over-priced cafés" – and, in ancient times, the notorious shenanigans of Tiberius gave it an enduring reputation as the ultimate in decadence, as did the party life here in the 1950s. Yet, if you choose to stay awhile, you will discover the real Capri beyond the hype – a world of traditional farm life, scenic hiking terrain and sparkling azure waters for swimming and boating. A place with undeniable allure for those who love the best of what life has to offer *(see pp28–9)*.

2 Ravello

This remarkable little town floats above the Amalfi Coast like a dream and has attracted its share of visionaries over the centuries, from artists to composers, to actors and philosophers. Notable visitors have included Richard Wagner, Franz Liszt, André Gide, D.H. Lawrence, Graham Greene and Gore Vidal, a current resident. Sumptuous palaces and their gardens, most now turned into exclusive hotels, recall Ravello's heyday centuries ago as a major mercantile centre and a political force to be reckoned with. But any visitor will be content simply with the astounding panoramas along the coast, that seem to stir the poetic inclinations in everyone who comes here *(see pp30–31)*.

3 Paestum

These ancient Greek temples are among the most complete – and most evocative – to have survived into modern times, even taking into account those in Greece itself. Besides the beauty and majesty of these timeless structures, this site has offered up countless other treasures, the remains of the Greco-Roman city that thrived here for some 1,000 years. The wonderful on-site museum is the repository of many unique finds, including the only known Greek paintings to have survived the ages. Taken from a tomb found nearby, the frescoes include a depiction of a joyous banquet of lovers, and a renowned diver – possibly a metaphor for the Greek conception of the afterlife *(see pp32–3)*.

Amalfi coastline, seen from Ravello

Hiking Spots

For all of its centuries of habitation, this region retains a great deal of virtually untouched natural beauty. On Capri, one of the best hikes is up the Scala Fenicia to Anacapri and then on up to the top of the island, Monte Solaro. On Ischia, the equivalent is to head up Via Monterone or Via Bocca from Forio, through the Falanga Forest to the summit of Monte Epomeo. Along the Amalfi Coast, the mule track above Positano, from Montepertuso to Nocella, offers stupendous views.

4 Ischia

The island of Ischia is surmounted by an extinct 788-m (2,585-ft) volcano, Monte Epomeo, and the many hot mineral springs here (some of them radioactive) have drawn cure- and pleasure-seekers to their soothing sources since ancient times. Green and rugged in appearance, the island also benefits from fine, long beaches. Like Capri, Ischia has had its share of famous residents – in the 19th century the Norwegian playwright Henrik Ibsen wrote *Peer Gynt* during a stay here, while in the 20th century the English poet W.H. Auden and his homosexual circle scandalized the locals. The island was also the first place in the area to be colonized by the Greeks, in the 8th century BC. *Map B4*

5 Procida

Smaller than Capri and Ischia and much less touristy, Procida attracts holiday-makers looking for tranquillity and cultural tradition. The island is flat with highly fertile soil, and is noted for its lemons, considered the best in the region. The island's most original feature, however, is its unique architecture. The colourful houses along the Chiaiolella Port, Marina Corricella and Marina di Sancio Cattolico are known for their vaults – built as winter boat shelters – arches and external staircases. *Map B4*

6 Vico Equense

On a rocky spur, Vico Equense is of Etruscan origin but was razed by the Goths in the 5th century. What is seen today, however, is the town's reinvention by the Angevin king of Naples in the 13th century. A visual high point is the church of Santissima Annunziata, dramatically perched atop a cliff that plunges straight down to the sea. *Map D4*

• *Santissima Annunziata: Open 9–10:30am Mon–Sat, 9am–12:30pm Sun; Free*

7 Sorrento

Palisades and grand hotels notwithstanding, there is no getting around the fact that Sorrento can be chaotic. Yet, popular in song and literature, the town has been a resort since the 1700s – Casanova and Goethe are two notable past visitors – and there is still charm to be found in the old streets. *Map D5*

Grand hotel, Sorrento

Massa Lubrense

8 Massa Lubrense

To the west of Sorrento, this is one of several fishing villages clustered around little ports. Rarely crowded, the site affords wonderful views across to Capri from the belvedere in Largo Vescovado. At Marina di Lobra there's a beach and a collection of pretty houses. *Map D5*

9 The Amalfi Coast

The famed *Costiera Amalfitana* lives up to the highest expectations in every way. The winding corniche road offers striking panoramas, and some of the towns seem to defy gravity clinging to impossibly steep slopes. Beauty and history are everywhere, tastefully blended with the *vita mondana* (sophisticated life) of Italian resorts. There's not much in the way of beaches, but on the whole, this perpendicular paradise never fails to delight. *Map E5*

10 Salerno

Renowned in medieval times for its medical school, this city has been almost entirely ignored by tourism. All that may change, however, now that the historic centre has undergone a restoration. The Romanesque Duomo and its treasures are a reminder that Salerno was the capital of southern Italy in the 11th century. *Map F4 • Duomo: Piazza Alfano I; Open 7:30am–8pm daily; Free*

A Day's Island Hopping

Morning

The tour begins on the island of **Procida**. To get there, take either the first hydrofoil from Naples-Beverello or Naples-Mergellina or the first ferry from Pozzuoli, all of which take about 35 minutes. You will arrive at Marina Grande, greeted by the sight of fishing boats and the colourful houses lining the port. Take a quick hike to the island's highest point, the Terra Murata ("walled town").

Back down on the marina, enjoy some refreshment at Bar Capriccio *(Via Roma 99)* while waiting for your hydrofoil to **Ischia**.

On Ischia you will arrive at Casamicciola, the island's second port, where you can have lunch at the wonderfully rustic Il Focolare *(Via Cretaio 68)*.

Afternoon

After lunch embark on a tour around the island in a glass-bottom boat (departs 2:30pm), stopping at the town of Sant'Angelo for an hour. Here you can take in the views, lounge by the dockside or walk along the cliff above Maronti Beach.

At the end of your tour, you can opt to stay over in one of the hotels in Casamicciola, or take a hydrofoil back to the mainland. If you spend the night, the next morning take the only hydrofoil of the day to **Capri** *(see pp28–9)* departing at 10:40am. After riding the funicular up to Capri Town, follow the signs up to the ruins of Villa Tiberius for the breathtaking view.

Following pages: **Sorrento coastline**

Left **Positano** Right **Duomo, Ravello**

TOP 10 Amalfi Coast Sights

1 Nerano

This quiet village, close to the tip of the peninsula, has views of the tiny archipelago that was known as Le Sirenuse. It was considered to be the home of the mythical Sirens, whose song lured mariners to their deaths on the rocks. *Map D5*

2 Positano

Known for decades as a smart playground for the wealthy, famous and decadent, Positano is an astonishingly vertical town in shades of pink and other faded pastels. Only one street snakes its way down and up – the rest are stairs. *Map E5*

3 Praiano

This little fishing village is perched on a ridge. Further along, you come to the Grotta dello Smeraldo (Emerald Cave). A lift takes you down to the boats to enter the grotto. *Map E5 • Grotta dello Smeraldo: Open Apr–Oct: 9am–4pm daily, Nov–Mar: 10am–3pm daily; Adm*

4 Amalfi

Amalfi is the largest and most historic town on its eponymous coastline. Between the 9th and 12th centuries the republic was at its height of mercantile power and the architecture still evokes that glory. The Duomo (cathedral) is glorious. *Map E5 • Duomo: Piazza del Duomo; Open Apr–Jun: 9am–7pm daily, Jul–Sep: 9am–9pm daily, Oct & Mar: 9:30am–5:15pm daily, Nov–Feb: 10am–1pm, 2:30–4:30pm daily; Free*

5 Atrani

This little town exudes a quiet charm, with arcades and a maze of alley-stairways. Its church of San Salvatore de' Bireto was where Amalfi's doges received their investiture. *Map E5 • San Salvatore de' Bireto: Closed for restoration*

6 Ravello

In the 13th century Ravello was an important player in the sea trade and the medieval look accounts for its captivating beauty *(see pp30–31)*.

7 Minori and Maiori

Maiori boasts the coast's longest beach, while Minori has the archaeological site, the Villa Romana *(see p101)*. *Map E5*

8 Cetara

Home to the most active fishing fleet on the coast, this is also the only place to buy *cola-tura di alici*, a fish sauce that is a descendent of the ancient Roman one called *garum*. *Map F4*

9 Vietri sul Mare

Vietri is universally known for its ceramics, begun in the 1400s and still deftly handcrafted and hand-painted. *Map F4*

10 Cava de' Tirreni

The main monument here is the 11th-century Badia della Santissima Trinità (Abbey of the Holy Trinity), housing paintings by De Matteis. *Map F4 • Abbey: Open 9am–12:30pm Mon–Sat, 9–10:30am Sun; Free*

Left **Villa Jovis, Capri** Right **Certosa de San Giacomo, Capri**

Top 10 Museums

1 Certosa de San Giacomo, Capri
This 14th-century monastery features North African-style vaults forming a series of little domes. It now houses the town's library. *Viale Certosa • Map U2 • Open 9am–2pm Tue–Sun • Free*

2 Villa Jovis, Capri
Very much in ruins, this Roman imperial palace's main attraction now lies in its stunning position *(see p28)*. *Via Tiberio • Map U1 • Open 9am–1 hour before sunset • Adm*

3 Villa San Michele, Anacapri
This villa contains ancient marbles and furnishings from the 17th to 19th centuries *(see p29)*. *Map T1 • Open 9am–1 hour before sunset • Adm*

4 Castello Aragonese, Ischia
In the 16th century poetess Vittoria Colonna held court here, making Ischia the cultural centre of the Mediterranean. Part of the ruin is now a hotel. *Map B4 • Open Mar–Nov: 9:30am–1 hour before sunset • Adm*

5 Area Archeologica de Santa Restituta, Ischia
Below the 10th century church lies an area where you can see remains of a 4th-century Christian basilica. *Piazza Santa Restituta, Lacco Ameno • Map A4 • Open Apr–Sep: 9:30am–12:30pm, 3:30–6pm Mon–Sat, 9:30am–12:30pm Sun • Adm*

6 Abbazia de San Michele Arcangelo, Procida
This 11th-century abbey is notable for its paintings by pupils of Luca Giordano. *Via Terra Murata 89 • Map B4 • Open 9:45am–12:45pm, 3–5pm Mon–Sat, 9:45am–12:45pm Sun • Adm*

7 Museo Antiquarium Equano, Vico Equense
Finds from this Roman town, now inside the town hall, consist of pottery, figurines and tools. *Casa Municipale, Via Filangieri 98 • Map D4 • Open 8:30am–12:30pm Mon, Wed, Fri; 8:30am–12:30pm, 4–6pm Tue, Thu • Free*

8 Correale di Terranova, Sorrento
In this 18th-century villa, archaeological finds include a 4th-century BC Greek original of Artemis on a Deer. *Via Correale 50 • Map D5 • Open 9am–2pm Wed–Mon • Adm*

9 Museo Archeologico Georges Vallet, Piano di Sorrento
This museum boasts finds from all over the peninsula, including pottery and weapons. *Via Ripa di Cassano 14 • Map D5 • Open 9am–1pm, 4–7pm Tue–Sun • Adm*

10 Villa Romana, Minori
In this aristocratic villa the fresco style dates from the 1st century AD. The antiquarium displays artifacts excavated here and at two sites nearby. *Via Capodipiazza 28 • Map E5 • Open 9am–1 hour before sunset • Free*

Left **Limonoro** Centre **L'Arco Antico** Right **Local ceramic dish**

TOP 10 Shopping

1 Sandalmakers, Capri
Cobblers jollier than these would be hard to find. Stop by to pick out designs you like and within a few hours – unless you choose something extra fancy – you'll have your very own hand-tooled, made-to-measure sandals. *Il Sandalo Caprese di Attilio: Via Sopramonte 9A; Map S1 • L'Arte del Sandal Caprese di Antonio Viva, Via G Orlandi 75, Anacapri; Map T1*

2 La Galleria dell'Arte, Anacapri
Some of the best ceramics on the island. Designs tend to evoke the natural hues of the setting – azure, gold, green – usually with flowers and vines or other florid vegetation. Anything can be designed to your specifications and you can watch the artists at work. *Via G Orlandi 105 • Map T1*

3 Corallium, Anacapri
A coral and cameo factory in Torre del Greco. The selection is extraordinary, created with both silver and gold, and prices are excellent. A certificate of guarantee comes with every purchase. *Via G Orlandi 163–5 • Map T1*

4 Limonoro, Sorrento
One of the top souvenirs from the area is *limoncello*, the signature lemon liqueur. This is a good place to see it being made, after which you'll know why it packs such a punch – it's basically pure alcohol with flavouring. *Via S Cesareo 51 • Map D5*

5 Salvatore Gargiulo, Sorrento
Examples of Sorrentine *intarsia* (marquetry) are to be seen all over town, but this workshop turns out top-quality products at reasonable prices. The best items are the music boxes. *Via Auoro 33 • Map D5*

6 Criscuolo, Amalfi
Here you'll find a little bit of everything, all of it head and shoulders above the usual tourist trinkets. Coral necklaces with silver baubles and lapis lazuli or turquoise are particularly appealing. *Largo Scario 6 • Map E5*

7 L'Arco Antico, Amalfi
L'Artico Antico helps keep Amalfi's tradition of handmade paper products alive. *Via P Capuano 4 • Map E5*

8 Capriccio, Ravello
A tiny, cave-like shop that specializes in contemporary ceramic art. *Piazza Duomo 6 • Map E4*

9 Ceramiche d'Arte, Ravello
This workshop is the place to come for gorgeous ceramics decorated with traditional designs. *Via dei Rufolo 16 • Map E4*

10 Ceramiche Solimene, Vietri sul Mare
Home to the world-famous Vietri dinnerware, where the bird design is used on plates, pitchers, sugar bowls – you name it. *Via Madonna degli Angeli 7 • Map F4*

Above **La Piazzetta, Capri**

Top 10 Nightlife

1 La Piazzetta, Capri

Capri Town's main square may be small but it's big on *la vita mondana* (sophisticated lifestyle). The little bars, with their cluster of outdoor tables, are a magnet for daytrippers and locals alike, although the latter turn up after dark after the former have moved on. ✆ *Map U1*

2 Taverna Anema e Core, Capri

The "Soul and Heart" taverna is still redolent of *la dolce vita* vibes of decades past and is considered Capri's premier nightclub. It attracts a chic, yet fun-loving crowd. ✆ *Via Sella Orta 39F • Map U1 • Closed Oct–Mar: Mon–Fri*

3 Numero Due, Capri

Another hot spot and local celebrity hangout. The DJ spins cool house and techno dance music, but don't get here before 2am. Dressy club attire is *de rigueur*. ✆ *Via Camerelle 1 • Map U1*

4 Underground, Anacapri

This disco-bar is a favourite with locals. Music includes hip-hop, funk and house. Live music is also sometimes on offer, with cabaret on Saturday nights. ✆ *Via G Orlandi 259 • Map T1*

5 Discoteca Valentino Pianobar, Ischia

This beautifully decorated club attracts a young, energetic crowd. ✆ *Corso Vittoria Colonna 97 • Map B4*

6 Pit Bull Irish Pub, Procida

Irish pubs have been popular in Italy for decades, and this one has excellent food, beers on tap, and great music, including live performers at times. ✆ *Via Roma 68, centre of Marina Grande • Map B4*

7 Artis Domus, Sorrento

You'll find both live music and disco here, in the cellar of a historic villa that belonged to a well-known Sorrentine poet and thinker. The atmosphere is terrific and there are excellent snacks too. ✆ *Via S Nicola 56 • Map D5*

8 Music on the Rocks, Positano

The weeknight attraction at this club, evocatively set inside a cavern, is the soulful sounds of the resident pianist Claudio Fiori. At weekends the place turns into a nightclub equipped with high-energy house and techno. Cover charge. ✆ *Grotta dell'Incanto 51 • Map E5 • Closed winter*

9 Africana, Marina di Praia

The approach to this disco is via a walkway excavated out of a seafront rock face, while the dance floor seems to be suspended above the waves. The decor includes ethnic masks and parrots. ✆ *Map E5*

10 RocoCò, Amalfi

Set up in the valley, this disco holds up to 200 party-goers. Good food available too. ✆ *Via delle Cartiere 98 • Map E5*

Left **Bar Tiberio** Right **Bar Ercolano**

TOP 10 Cafés and Gelaterie

1 Bar Tiberio, Capri
One of the main bars on the renowned Piazzetta, but everyone has his or her own favourite. Great for people-watching. *La Piazzetta • Map U1*

2 Aumm Aumm, Anacapri
A favourite among both local youth and visitors, this little bar doubles as a club, sandwich shop and *pizzeria*, open until late. Don't overlook the excellent desserts. *Via Caprile 2 • Map T1*

3 Bar Calise, Ischia
One of the island's best bars, with excellent *gelato* (ice cream) and *dolci* (desserts). It's surrounded by dense greenery in the middle of a traffic circle in this laid-back port. *Piazza degli Eroi 69 • Map B4*

4 Bar Stany & Elio, Ischia
Named after the Italian monikers for old-time slapstick comedians Stan Laurel and Oliver Hardy, who have always had a fervent following in this country. It's centrally located and features great *gelato*, made on the premises. *Via Castellaccio 77, Forio • Map A4*

5 Dal Cavaliere, Procida
The clientele here are definitely upper-crust – tending towards yachting types and Neapolitan high-rollers. Great *granita al limone* (lemon iced sorbet), among other sweet treats. *Via Roma 42–3 • Map B4*

6 Bar Ercolano, Sorrento
Located in what is probably the best people-watching piazza in town, this elegant little bar has the requisite cluster of outdoor tables from which to ogle the crowds. After 8pm, most of the area is closed to traffic. *Piazza Tasso • Map D5*

7 La Zagara, Positano
A major tourist magnet, but there's no denying that the treats they turn out here are delicious: pastries, cakes, fresh fruit sorbets and the like. The patio, with fragrant lemon trees, is captivating. *Via dei Mulini 6 • Map E5*

8 Il Doge d'Amalfi, Amalfi
Inside, the place is elegant; outside the tables provide a view of the Duomo and the goings-on in the square. The sandwiches come in tempting variations and there are lots of delicious sweets too. *Piazza Duomo 2 • Map E5*

9 Casbah'r, Atrani
This bar-restaurant has vibrant decor inside and tables out under the arcades or in the sunny square. Internet connections also possible. *Piazza Umberto I • Map E5*

10 Bar Anna, Paestum
A family-run place for either a drink or more substantial fare. A good chance to try the local *mozzarella di bufala*, either in a salad or in a *panino* (sandwich). *Via Magna Grecia 841 • Map H6*

Above **Da Gemma**

Price Categories

For a three-course meal for one with half a bottle of wine (or equivalent meal), taxes and extra charges.

€	under €20
€€	€20–€30
€€€	€30–€40
€€€€	€40–€50
€€€€€	over €50

Top 10 Pizzerias

1 Da Gemma, Capri

Off a covered arcade just up from the Piazzetta, this place is a Capri institution. There's usually an enticing buffet spread, as well as good pizzas and great views. *Via Madre Serfina 6 • Map U1 • 081 837 04 61 • Closed Mon • €€*

2 Villa Verde, Capri

Offering spacious indoor seating as well as a lush garden with a fountain and a grotto, this restaurant has exquisite *focaccia* and pizza and an excellent house red from Calabria. *Via Sella Orta 6/a • Map U1 • 081 837 70 24 • €€*

3 Da Pasquale, Sant'Angelo, Ischia

Dining is home-style here, even to the occasional sharing of tables and bench seating. The pizza is good and there's a reasonable choice of beer and wine. *Via Sant'Angelo 79 • Map B4 • 081 90 42 08 • No credit cards • €*

4 Da Michele 36, Procida

A favourite with locals. The pizza does not disappoint, and there are good wines too. *Molo di Levante, Via Roma 1 • Map B4 • 081 896 78 86 • €€*

5 Gigino Pizza al Metro, Vico Equense

"Pizza by the metre" means they'll go to any length to fulfill your order, whether it's a bus-load of tourists or a family of any size. *Via Nicotera 15 • Map D4 • 081 879 84 26 • No credit cards • €*

6 Sant'Antonio, Sorrento

Excellent, wood-fired pizza is served here for both lunch and dinner. The advantage of traditional wood ovens is that the heat flash-bakes the dough, preventing the toppings from becoming soggy. *Via Santa Maria delle Grazie 6 • Map D5 • 081 877 12 00 • €*

7 La Brace, Praiano

More Neapolitan-style pizzas from wood-fired ovens. In addition, you'll find a good selection of seafood, either grilled or combined with pasta. *Via Gennaro Capriglione 146 • Map E5 • 089 87 42 26 • €€€*

8 Da Maria, Amalfi

To complement your wood-fired pizza here you are automatically served a basket of garlic bread. *Via Lorenzo d'Amalfi 14 • Map E5 • 089 87 18 80 • Closed Mon • €€*

9 Pizzeria Vicolo della Neve, Salerno

Delicious pizza, as well as *pasta e fagioli* (with beans) and their signature dish *cianfotta* (mixed vegetables with bacon). *Vicolo della Neve 24 • Map F4 • 089 22 57 05 • Closed L, Wed • No credit cards • €*

10 Nonna Scepa, Paestum

The least touristy of the choices here turns out excellent pizzas, as well as seafood and other home-style dishes. Wild mushrooms in season – try some on your pizza. *Via Laura 53 • Map H6 • 082 885 10 64 • €€*

***Note:** Unless otherwise stated, all restaurants accept credit cards and serve vegetarian meals*

Left **La Savardina "da Edoardo"** Right **Swordfish, Alberto al Mare**

Top 10 Island Dining

1 Buca di Bacco "da Serafina", Capri

This lively, welcoming place is top of most locals' list, for both quality and price. The cooking features seafood, *antipasti* and pizzas. *Via Longano 35 • Map U1 • 081 837 07 23 • Closed Wed • €€€*

2 Aisha, Capri

Every week the menu is different here, but expect such creations as warm rabbit salad or saffron ravioli with salmon. *Gradoni Sopramonte 6 • Map U1 • 081 837 90 54 • Closed L, Mon • €€€*

3 La Savardina "da Edoardo", Capri

A beautiful spot, set amid citrus trees, serves traditional home-cooking using fresh ingredients from the garden. *Via Lo Capo 8 • Map U1 • 081 837 63 00 • €€*

4 Il Solitario, Anacapri

Hidden away down a narrow walkway, this delightful place is like being in someone's private garden. Everything is homemade and the freshest the season has to offer. *Via G Orlandi 96 • Map T1 • 081 837 07 32 • €€*

5 Il Cucciolo, Anacapri

This terrace-restaurant enjoys views of the sea and the bay, and the food is divine. Since it is out of the way, call and they'll pick you up, wherever on the island you may be. *Nuova Traversa Veterino 50 or Via La Fabbrica 52 • Map T1 • 081 837 19 17 • €€€*

6 Alberto al Mare, Ischia

Located over the water, the bounty of the sea is, naturally, the speciality here. Options might include *pesce spada* (swordfish) or *coda di rospo* (monkfish). *Via Cristoforo Colombo 8 • Map B4 • 081 98 12 59 • €€€*

7 Il Melograno, Ischia

A Michelin star winner, seafood is the keynote here, from fish *carpaccio* (raw or marinated) to grilled whole fish right off the boat. *Via G Mazzella 110 • Map B4 • 081 99 84 50 • €€€€*

8 Lo Scoglio, Sant'Angelo, Ischia

This restaurant, overlooking an illuminated cove, is carved out of a rock formation. Delicious fresh seafood. *Via Cava Ruffano 58 • Map B4 • 081 99 95 29 • €€*

9 La Medusa, Procida

More seafood, including a perennial favourite, *zuppa di pesce* (fish soup). For the more adventurous, there's spaghetti with *ricci di mare* (sea urchins). *Via Roma 116 • Map B4 • 081 896 74 81 • €€*

10 La Conchiglia, Chiaia Beach, Procida

Get here by walking down 183 steps from Piazza Olmo or reserve a boat trip. Once here, try pasta with *fiori di zucca* (squash blossoms), crab, cream and clams, finishing off with a lime liqueur. *Steps from Via Pizzaco 10 • Map B4 • 081 896 76 02 • €€€*

Above **Da Emilia**

Price Categories

For a three-course meal for one with half a bottle of wine (or equivalent meal), taxes and extra charges.	€	under €20
	€€	€20–€30
	€€€	€30–€40
	€€€€	€40–€50
	€€€€€	over €50

Top 10 Peninsula Dining

1 Torre del Saraceno, Marina di Equa

Well deserving of its Michelin star. *Antipasti* choices include sea urchins or caviar; all pastas are made on the premises; and the fresh fish melts in your mouth. *Via Torretta 9 • Map D5 • 081 802 85 55 • €€€€*

2 Ristorante Vittoria, Sorrento

The grandest experience Sorrento has to offer, in the glittering frescoed dining room of this superlative hotel. Silver, china, crystal and fine linen complement the service you receive. Former diners have included Goethe, Byron, Wagnor, Princess Margaret and Pavarotti. *Grand Hotel Excelsior Vittoria, Piazza Tasso 34 • Map D5 • 081 807 10 44 • €€€€*

3 Da Emilia, Sorrento

A family-run, unpretentious place serving good, traditional food. Tables on the terrace overlook the sea. *Via Marina Grande 62 • Map D5 • 081 807 27 20 • No credit cards • €€*

4 Don Alfonso 1890, Sant'Agata sui Due Golfi, Sorrentine Peninsula

With three Michelin stars expect lavish elegance and impeccable food. Tasting menus and their accompanying wines reach such heights that the effect is nothing less than symphonic. *Corso Sant'Agata 13 • Map D5 • 081 878 00 26 • Closed Mon • €€€€€*

5 La Cambusa, Positano

Positioned to the right of the beach, with dining on a porticoed balcony. Seafood is the thing to go for. *Piazza Vespucci 4 • Map E5 • 089 87 54 32 • Closed Tue • €€€€*

6 Il Capitano, Positano

Dishes include *ravioli di astice* (lobster-stuffed), while the *sommelier* will be happy to guide you through the wine list. Book ahead. *Via Pasitea 119 • Map E5 • 089 81 13 51 • Open Wed D only • €€€€*

7 Marina Grande, Amalfi

One of the best restaurants in town, set right on the sea. Original dishes include seafood ravioli with *arugula* (rocket) sauce. *Viale delle Regioni • Map E5 • 089 87 11 29 • €€€*

8 Casbah'r, Atrani

Dishes vary depending on the season, but expect such creations as pumpkin with baby squid or salt-cod *(see p104)*.

9 Villa Amore, Ravello

A breathtaking setting and traditional food. *Via dei Fusco 5 • Map E4 • 089 85 71 35 • €€*

10 Salvatore, Ravello

A short walk out of town, this restaurant enjoys a fine panorama and turns out delicious food. Try cuttlefish with artichokes or risotto of barley with mushrooms and smoked mozzarella. *Via della Repubblica 2 • Map E4 • 089 85 72 27 • €€€*

***Note:** Unless otherwise stated, all restaurants accept credit cards and serve vegetarian meals*

Left **Marechiaro** Right **Anfiteatro Flavio**

Posillipo, Pozzuoli and the North

IF CENTRAL SEASIDE NAPLES IS KNOWN AS "ROYAL NAPLES", *the coastal area to the west could be called "Imperial Naples" for its enormous popularity with imperial families and their courtiers in ancient Roman times. Significant ruins left by them are everywhere you look (as well as inland to the north) hiding behind the postwar* abusivo *(illegal) building developments that now blot the landscape. However, the entire area is subject to one of nature's stranger phenomena, called Bradyseism – underground volcanic activity gives rise to "slow earthquakes", resulting in the continual rising and lowering of the land, making it a rather unstable base for settlement. The region is relatively unexplored by modern-day tourists but was top of the list for those who took the 19th-century Grand Tour, not least because it includes one of Italy's finest palaces, the Reggia di Caserta, dating from the 18th century.*

Statue, Reggia di Caserta

TOP 10 Sights

1. Capo Posillipo
2. Marechiaro
3. Parco Virgiliano
4. Pozzuoli
5. Anfiteatro Flavio
6. Baia
7. Parco Archeologico e Monumentale di Baia
8. Museo Archeologico dei Campi Flegrei
9. Cumae
10. Reggia di Caserta

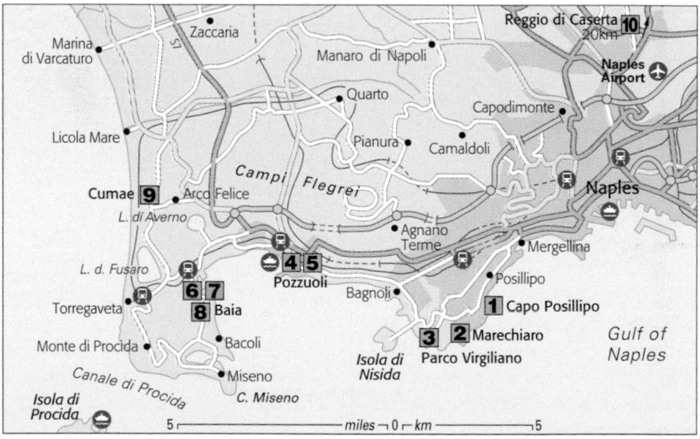

1 Capo Posillipo

The ancient Greeks called the area *Pausilypon* ("respite from pain") due to the great beauty of the place. Down through the ages, it retained its appeal through a succession of inhabitants and visitors, from religious communities in medieval times to holiday resorts for the Spanish aristocracy in the 17th century. The spartan years of the 1950s, however, finally put an end to that famous beauty in large swaths with the unregulated spread of ugly apartment buildings. Fortunately, parts of the area down by the water still retain considerable charm, mainly the 17th-century Villa Volpicelli, appearing like a floating castle at the water's edge. *Map J2*

2 Marechiaro

Long considered one of the most romantic spots on this evocative coastline, this little fishing village remains a popular destination, with ancient ruins and restaurants with great views. The panoramic vista of Vesuvius from here has been repeatedly celebrated, most nostalgically in that quintessential Neapolitan song "O Sole Mio". *Map J2*

3 Parco Virgiliano

Occupying the summit of a large hill overlooking the sea, this park offers spectacular views on all sides. To the left, the Bay of Naples, Vesuvius and the Sorrentine Peninsula; to the right, the Bay of Pozzuoli and the Phlegrean Fields. Down below lies the little island of Nisida, formed from an ancient volcanic crater. The tomb of the epic poet Virgil is said to be here in the ruins of a *columbarium* (sepulchre) used by ancient Romans to house the ashes of the dead.
Salita della Grotta 20 • Map J2 • Open 9am–1 hour before sunset daily • Free

4 Pozzuoli

Called Puteoli by the Romans, this now modest seaside town was a major player 2,000 years ago. It is rife with significant ruins, including the *Serapeum*, thought for centuries to be a temple of the Egyptian god Serapis but now known to have been one of the empire's largest markets. Puteoli was the main imperial port and retained its importance even after the Port of Ostia, at the mouth of the Tiber, was upgraded by Emperor Trajan in the 2nd century. *Map C3*

Serapeum, Pozzuoli

Ancient ruins, Baia

5 Anfiteatro Flavio

This is the third-largest Roman amphitheatre in the world, after those at Rome and Capua – again making it clear how important this area was to the empire. It had a seating capacity of 40,000 and was equipped with an array of below-floor apparatus for making the *venationes* (wild animal "hunts") that took place here as theatrical as possible. Nowhere are such systems so well preserved, thanks to the lower portion of the structure having been buried until modern times. *Via Terracciano 75 • Map C3 • Open 9am–1 hour before sunset • Adm*

6 Baia

This little town was the most sumptuous resort of the ancient world – everyone who was anyone had a seaside retreat of daunting size and opulent luxury here. Due to the seismic activity in this area, however, much of the land and the structures are now underwater, forming a unique flooded city that can be explored by dives or by boat. There's also a 15th-century castle here, the Castello di Baia, housing an archaeological museum, while to the north is Lago d'Averno, a crater lake that the ancients believed marked the entrance to the Underworld. *Map B3*
• Underwater City: Associazione Aliseo, Piazza della Repubblica 42; Tours mid-Mar–Nov: noon & 4pm Sat, 10:30am, noon, 4pm Sun; Adm

The Burning Fields

Flegrei and Phlegrean derive from a Greek word *phlegraios* (burning), applied in ancient times to this zone of perpetual, low-level volcanic activity. Below the earth's surface here, magma (molten rock) is flowing, applying pressure upward, making it one of the most unstable regions of the earth's crust, literally littered with volcanic cones and craters.

7 Parco Archeologico e Monumentale di Baia

Arranged in terraces, this excavated area includes an ancient spa and a Temple of Diana. The spa complex comprises baths named after Venus and Mercury, the latter a large swimming pool once covered with a dome. *Via Fusaro 75 • Map B3 • Open 9am–1 hour before sunset • Adm*

8 Museo Archeologico dei Campi Flegrei

The area's archaeological museum contains a reassembled *sacellum* (shrine) featuring statues of several emperors. There's also a reconstruction of a *nymphaeum* (fountain), the original of which still lies under 6 m (20 ft) of water. Its statues have been raised, however, and illustrate the story of how Ulysses and his men escaped from the Cyclops Polyphemus. *Via Castello 39, Bacoli • Map B3 • Open 9am–1 hour before sunset Tue–Sun • Adm*

9 Cumae

Cumae was founded in the 8th century BC and played a significant part in history, due to its resident seeress. The Cumaean Sibyl, priestess of Apollo and similar to her counterpart at Delphi, was an oracle who exerted great influence, and the leaders of Rome depended on her prophecies and guidance in times of crisis. A visit to the Sibyl's Grotto, with its weird trapezoidal entrance tunnel, remains an enigmatic experience.

Via Montecuma • Map B3 • Open 9am–1 hour before sunset daily • Adm

10 Reggia di Caserta

This 18th-century palace was built by the Bourbons. Neapolitan Baroque at its most refined, it is built around four courtyards and has 1,200 lavish rooms. Highlights include the Great Staircase and the Throne Room. The park has a number of huge fountains, decorated with statuary, culminating in the Grande Cascata, plummeting 78 m (255 ft).

Via Douet 2 • Map D1 • Palace: Open 8:30am–7:30pm Tue–Sun • Museum: Open 9am–1pm Tue–Sun • Park: 9am–1 hour before sunset Tue–Sun • Adm

Throne Room, Reggia di Caserta

A Morning in Ancient Pozzuoli

Start the tour in the cool of the morning with a visit to Solfatara (opens 8:30am), the vast volcanic lava cap about 1 km (0.5 mile) north of the town. This stark, bizarre site will set the tone for the day's musings on the ephemeral nature of all things. Next, head back towards town on the Via Vecchia di San Gennaro and take a quick left on Via Domiziana, which follows the ancient Roman road of basalt stones built to link Rome to Puteoli (Pozzuoli). Visit the Santuario di San Gennaro and see the spot where Naples' patron saint met his martyrdom under Emperor Diocletian.

From here, turn back and go down Via Vecchia di San Gennaro to the Piscina Cardito, a 2nd-century cistern with a vaulted ceiling supported by pillars. Continue on to the great **Anfiteatro Flavio** and try to imagine what it might have been like, with full scenery and exotic beasts springing out of trapdoors. Next, follow Via Terracciano along to the Terme di Nettuno, huge terraced baths, and on the opposite slope the Ninfeo di Diana, a fountain that may have been part of the baths.

Work your way down towards the ancient port, most of it now underwater, to the *Serapeum* (market). Walk up onto the promontory, the Rione Terra, to visit the 2,000-year-old Duomo (cathedral).

Finally, enjoy a well-deserved lunch at the **Antica Trattoria da Ciuffello** *(see p113)*.

On the tour of Pozzuoli make sure you bring bottles of water and protection from the sun.

Left **Palazzo Donn'Anna** Right **Santa Maria del Faro**

TOP 10 Best of the Rest

1 Palazzo Donn'Anna, Posillipo
The air of mystery that envelops this 17th-century palace has given rise to various rumours. One claims that Queen Joan II used it for illicit trysts, after which she had her lovers tossed into the sea. *Piazza Donn'Anna 9 • Map J2 • Closed to the public*

2 Santa Maria del Faro, Posillipo
Dating back to the 1300s, this church was probably built over the remains of a Roman *faro* (lighthouse). It was restored in the 18th century. *Via Marechiaro 96a • Map J2 • Open during services*

3 War Memorial Mausoleo, Posillipo
This Votive Altar is dedicated to the lost lives of World War I. The astonishing structure shows caryatids gazing as if possessed by grief. *Map J2 • Open 7am–noon Tue–Sun*

4 Science City, Posillipo
This hands-on science centre is designed to educate and entertain kids of all ages *(see p56)*. *Via Coroglio 104 • Map J2 • Open 9am–5pm Tue–Sat; 10am–7pm Sun • Adm*

5 Astroni
The Romans tapped the geothermal properties of this extinct volcanic crater to build spas. *Riserva degli Astroni, Agnano • Map C3 • Open 9:30am–4:30pm daily • Adm*

6 Solfatara, Pozzuoli
Located just above the town, another crater of a dormant volcano presents an otherworldly landscape. It was called the *Forum Vulcani* (Vulcan's Forum) by the Romans, who also found its sulphurous spewings fascinating. *Via Solfatara 161 • Map C3 • Open 8:30am–1 hour before sunset daily • Adm*

7 Santuario di San Gennaro, Pozzuoli
This 16th-century church is said to mark the spot where Naples' patron saint was decapitated, and the brown stain on a stone here is said to be his blood. *Via S Gennaro Agnano 10 • Map C3 • Open 8am–noon, 4:30–8pm Mon–Sat; 8am–1pm, 4:30–8pm Sun • Free*

8 Bacoli
One of the chief marvels here is the *Piscina Mirabile*, a cistern used to collect water for the ancient port of Misenum. *Via A Greco 10 • Map B3 • Open 9am–1 hour before sunset daily • Free*

9 Santa Maria Capuavetere
The Appian Way, the first Roman highway, led south to Capua, the "biggest and richest city in Italy", according to Livy in the 1st century BC. *Map C1*

10 Benevento
This town's pride and joy is the well-preserved Arch of Trajan, chronicling the Roman emperor's civic works. *Map F1*

Price Categories

For a three-course meal for one with half a bottle of wine (or equivalent meal), taxes and extra charges.	€	under €20
	€€	€20–€30
	€€€	€30–€40
	€€€€	€40–€50
	€€€€€	over €50

Above **Gelateria Bilancione**

Top 10 Places to Eat

1 Gelateria Bilancione, Posillipo

Choose your favourite *gelato* at this traditional ice cream shop and then head across the street to enjoy it sitting on a bench taking in the vista. *Via Posillipo 238B • Map J2*

2 Al Faretto, Posillipo

This seafood restaurant is known for its romantic atmosphere and wonderful views. The catches of the day are served up in sumptuous style. *Porticciolo do Marechiaro • Map J2 • 081 575 04 07 • Closed Mon, 1 week in Aug • €€€*

3 Giuseppone a Mare, Posillipo

More excellent seafood here, renowned since 1889. Popular for receptions and celebrations, so book ahead. *Via Russo 13 • Map J2 • 081 769 13 84 • Closed Mon, Sun L, 2 weeks in Aug • €€€€*

4 Antica Trattoria da Cluffello, Pozzuoli

Overlooking the central piazza, this restaurant is well known for its grilled specialities. Their consummate *zuppa di pesce* (fish soup) is a meal all in itself. *Via Dicearchia 11 bis • Map C3 • 081 526 00 07 • Closed Mon (winter) • €€€*

5 La Ninfea, Pozzuoli

A speciality here is *schiaffoni alla ninfea*, a delicious seafood pasta dish. *Via Lago Lucrino • Map C3 • 081 866 13 26 • No credit cards • €€€*

6 Il Casolare da Tobia, Baia

Wonderful organically grown food, from the rich volcanic soil of the crater on which the place is perched. *Via Selvatico 12 • Map B3 • 081 523 51 93 • No credit cards • No vegetarian options • €€*

7 Anfiteatro Cumano, Cumae

Dine either inside or on the terrace in the garden. For a delicious experience, try the *linguine alla marinara* (egg pasta with seafood). *Via Cuma 576 • Map B3 • 081 854 31 19 • Closed Tue • No credit cards • €€*

8 Féfé, Bacoli

Filled with regulars, this place faces the port. Once you get a table, you are welcomed with the house aperitif and advised of the seafood specials of the day. *Via Miseno 137, Case Vecchie • Map B3 • 081 523 30 11 • Closed Mon–Fri L, Mon D (winter) • €€*

9 Leucio, Casertavecchia-San Leucio

A 10-minute drive north of Caserta. Try *risotto vergine*, with squid, prawns and cuttlefish. *Strada Panoramica • Map D1 • 082 330 12 41 • Closed Mon, Sun D • €€*

10 Teatro Gastronomico, Benevento

This showy place features decor reminiscent of ancient Roman wall paintings – complete with *trompe-l'oeil* scenery. Good value. *Via Traiano 65 • Map F1 • 082 45 46 05 • Closed Mon, Sun D • €€*

***Note:** Unless otherwise stated, all restaurants accept credit cards and serve vegetarian meals*

8
SEPPIE

STREETSMART

Information & Planning 116

Getting to Naples 117

Getting Around 118

Things to Avoid 119

Security & Health 120

Banking & Communications 121

Family & Budget Tips 122

Special Concerns 123

Accommodation Tips 124

Places to Stay 125–133

Left **Amalfi Coast in summer** Right **Tourist information sign**

TOP 10 Information & Planning

1 Internet Information

A number of general websites can help you research exactly which parts and how much of this fascinating area you want to cover during your visit. Bear in mind that the official, locally tended sites are mostly in Italian only. *www.italiantourism.com • naplesit.ags.myareaguide.com • www.capriweb.com • www.enit.it • www.deliciousitaly.com*

2 Climate

July and August are relentlessly hot and humid, with temperatures around 30°–40°C (85°–105°F), in addition to which most of Italy will be on holiday with you. The best weather is generally found in spring and autumn. Rain can definitely come into the picture in March, April and September. Winter months can be cold, dark and rainy, but with clear views of Vesuvius dusted with snow.

3 When to Go

For culture, go in the winter, when you'll get a real feel for local life. For swimming, you can't avoid the hot months, but to side-step the crowds, September is a better bet than July and August. For appreciating the sheer beauty of the natural setting and the quality of life, any time of year is ideal.

4 Visas

Citizens of the EU, the US, Australia, New Zealand, Canada and Japan need no visa for stays of up to three months. For longer stays you should apply at the local *questura* (police station) for a *permesso di soggiorno*. Other nationalities should check entry details at their local embassy or consulate.

5 Italian Consulates

Italian consulates in your home country can be good sources of more detailed information, including tourism, employment and residency in Italy. *UK: 38 Eaton Place, London, 020 7235 9371 • USA: 690 Park Ave, New York, 212 737 9100 • Canada: 136 Beverley St, Toronto, 416 977 1566 • Australia: Level 45, Macquarie Place, Sydney, 029 392 7900 • Ireland: 63–5 Northumberland Rd, Dublin, 01 660 1744*

6 Italian National Tourist Offices

For brochures, maps and upcoming events, contact the Italian Tourist Board in your home country. *UK: 1 Princes St, London, 020 7408 1254 • USA: 630 5th Ave, Suite 1565, New York, 212 245 4822 • Canada: 1 Place Ville Marie, Suite 1914, Montréal, Quebec, 514 866 7667 • Australia: c/o Italian Embassy, Level 43, Macquarie Place, Sydney, 029 392 7900*

7 Tourist Offices

Offices of the *Azienda Autonoma di Soggiorno* (ASST) will provide you with free maps and brochures. Other tourist offices, run by the *Ente Provinciale del Turismo* (EPT), are located in key spots. *ASST: Via S Carlo 9; 081 40 23 94; Piazza del Gesù; 081 552 33 28 • EPT: Mergellina Train Station, 081 761 21 02; Piazza dei Martiri 58, Chiaia, 081 40 53 11*

8 General Information

Italy is on GMT + 1 hour; daylight saving time is observed from spring to autumn. Electricity is 220V and outlets require plugs with two round prongs, so you may need an adapter and a transformer.

9 Insurance

EU nationals are automatically entitled to medical care in Italy, but will need the E111 form available from post offices. Other nationalities should take out travel insurance, to cover both health and property.

10 What to Take

Top on the list should be a good sunscreen. Any prescription or non-prescription medicines you may require should also go into your carry-on bag. Italian pharmacies are very helpful, but drugs may go by unrecognizable names.

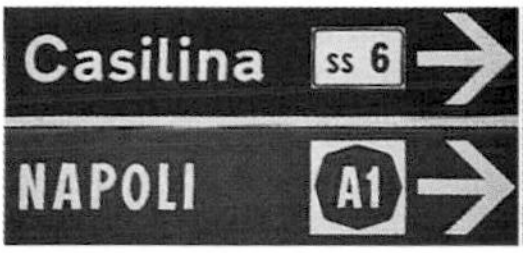

Left **Road signs** Right **Coastal ferry**

Getting to Naples

1 By Air from Europe

Naples' airport is linked to all major Italian cities and many European ones. Airlines that fly from the UK include British Airways and easyJet. Alitalia is the main carrier within Italy. *British Airways: 199 712 266; www.britishairways.com • easyJet: www.easyjet.com • Alitalia: 848 865 643; www.alitalia.it*

2 By Intercontinental Air

There are few intercontinental flights to Naples. Most visitors fly to Rome and then connect by air or land. The airport is located just 8 km (5 miles) from the central train station and about twice that distance from the ferry and hydrofoil ports. Bus services into town are available, as are taxis. *Capodichino Airport: 081 789 61 11*

3 Charter Flights and Deals

Travel agents have access to systems that will enable you to compare deals offered by different charter airlines. However, specials offered by major airlines can often be cheaper than those of the budget carriers.

4 Packages

Given the glamorous port destinations, cruise packages are very popular, as are land packages that focus on the archaeological and cultural themes. The advantage of package tours is that everything is seen to, allowing you to keep at arm's length from potential confusion when encountering the local way of life.

5 By Car

Reaching the area by car is possible but it is by no means advisable for the uninitiated. As you hit Naples, there are so many perplexing interchanges, with inadequate signage, that most newcomers will find themselves promptly lost.

6 By Sea

If you are coming to the area from Sardinia, Sicily, the Aeolian Islands, other Mediterranean ports, or on a cruise, this mode is a pleasant option, either by ferry or hydrofoil. You will see all the beauties of the bay and receive an impression of Naples at its most sophisticated. *Tirrenia: 081 720 11 11 • Siremar: 081 580 03 40 • SNAV: 081 761 23 48*

7 By Bus

Regular buses and coaches are a reasonable way to get to Naples and other towns in the area. If arriving by bus in Naples you will find yourself in one of the main squares, Piazza Garibaldi, in front of the train station.

8 Trains

EuroStar trains, introduced some years ago, are now the only ones that have any chance of arriving on time, since they are given precedence over all others when track tie-ups occur. Most stop at both Mergellina and Garibaldi stations. All other services are options, but expect delays. The journey time from Rome to Naples by train is between two and three hours. *Ferrovia dello Stato: 848 888 088; www.trenitalia.com*

9 Car Rental

The minimum age for renting a car is 25, and most companies require that you be covered for any eventual problem, including collision damage and theft. But again, driving in this region is not particularly recommended for novices or nervous drivers. *Hertz: 199 112 211; www.hertz.it • Avis: 199 100 133; www.avis.com • Europcar: 800 014 410; www.europcar.com • Maggiore-Budget: 848 867 067; www.maggiore.it*

10 Motorbike

If you are doing Italy on a two-wheeler, be sure to travel south via the coast road down from Rome, which avoids the erratic madness and unpredictability of driving on Italian *autostrade* (motorways).

P&O Cruises (www.pocruises.co.uk) offer packages that call in at Naples; for luxury cruises see www.windstarcruises.com

Left **Naples bus** Right **Taxi**

TOP 10 Getting Around

1 Walking
The main sights of central Naples are close enough to each other that walking is the top choice for getting around. In the old quarter, it's really the only practical choice. Bring a sturdy pair of shoes, however, that provide solid support on the uneven pavements and cobbles.

2 By Bus
The city buses in Naples are not for the faint-hearted. The system is chaotic and the old buses are dirty, crowded and subject to traffic jams. Most bus lines have their terminus at Piazza Garibaldi. Buy tickets from any local bar before boarding.

3 By Train & Tram
Naples and its vicinity has a complex but reliable system of trains, including trams, funicular railways and three local light railways that serve outlying areas. Trams run along the shore and the funiculars go up to Vomero, while the Circumvesuviana goes all the way to Sorrento, with many stops along the way, including the major archaeological sites such as Pompeii. The Cumana and Circumflegreo go west to the Campi Flegrei. There's also a metro system, and most of these lines converge conveniently at the central station.

4 By Car
For most, getting around the area by car is likely to stress even the calmest of drivers – private cars are not allowed on Capri, traffic jams on the Sorrentine Peninsula and the Amalfi Coast are maddening, car theft is common, and the motorways are chaotic.

5 By Motorcycle
This is a fine idea for getting around Ischia, and possibly the archaeological areas west of Naples, but elsewhere you will run into the same problems as you would by car. Narrow, curving roads lined with too many vehicles are the major problems.

6 By Boat
It's conceivable that, once here, you could stick to hydrofoils, going from port to port – Naples has two, then there are the islands, Pozzuoli, Sorrento, Positano, Amalfi and Salerno – and doing your sightseeing entirely on foot. By private boat, of course, your options increase enormously.

7 By Taxi
Almost without exception, taxi drivers in Naples are dishonest and will try to find ways to increase your tab shamelessly. A favourite trick is to fiddle the meter so that it charges the rate for out-of-town travel, or they simply invent "surcharges". It's always best to spend a moment settling the cost of the trip in advance, meter or no meter, especially with lengthy waits in traffic.

8 By Bicycle
The driving in Naples and any built-up area is far too crazy to allow for safe bicycle travel. However, it's a definite option on the islands of Procida and Ischia, as well as on some of the mountainous backroads along the Sorrentine Peninsula and remoter areas west of Naples.

9 Kayaking
On the islands, there's no better way to really get to know the secrets of the shoreline and the smaller grottoes than to rent your own kayak. You can circumnavigate Capri, for example, in about 4 or 5 hours, including stops for a swim at secluded spots. Take a supply of drinking water and slather on waterproof sunscreen beforehand.

10 Hiking
This area is blessed with scenic mountain trails, especially on Ischia and Capri and above Positano and Amalfi. Some of them thread their way along old goat paths from village to village, often with the reward of a wonderful restaurant at the end.

Circumvesuviana trains to Pompeii are frequent. They depart from Stazione Centrale and take around 30 minutes.

Left **Seafood** Right **Hair-raising road**

Top 10 Things to Avoid

1 Pollution

As lovely as the Bay of Naples is, parts of it are quite polluted and you should heed warning signs. If an area is posted *"vietato"* it is probably not safe to swim or fish there. Air pollution can also be a problem in hot, dry seasons in Naples proper, so anyone who suffers from respiratory conditions should bring along suitable medication. The tap water is usually safe to drink but, in general, bottled water will taste better.

2 Spoiled Food

In hot weather always choose reputable-looking bars and restaurants if you plan on having anything to eat that involves mayonnaise or fish of any kind. Food-poisoning is not a common problem here, but eating things that have gone off can spoil your holiday faster than almost any other factor.

3 Bad Manners

When visiting churches remember to dress respectfully and to conduct yourself in a quiet manner that will not offend any worshippers who may be present. This is extremely important during services of any kind – weddings and masses, for example – when many churches discourage sightseers altogether.

4 Pickpockets

Wherever there are crowds, there are pickpockets. This includes trains, subways, buses, hydrofoils, streets and museums. Such petty thieves are very shrewd and know how to attack when you are most vulnerable – especially when getting on or off a bus or when you're in a hurry and your attention is elsewhere. The best rule is simply to carry all valuables under your clothing, or in zipped-up inside pockets, where easy access is denied. Clutch bags and wallets firmly to your front.

5 Short-Change Artists

Count your change and examine all bills, especially restaurant tabs. Taxi drivers may also try to give you insufficient change, so don't rush out of the cab when you reach your destination. Take time to make sure you were dealt with fairly and properly – most people you encounter will be honest, but it's your responsibility too to make sure you are not cheated.

6 Beggars

Most beggars simply sit on the steps of a church or on a street with their hand out. Few try to make a nuisance of themselves, but if they do, a firm *"no"* will give the right message.

7 Swindles

Shell games and such attract a crowd in large squares. Although it might be fun to watch, do not get involved – these games are fixed.

8 Peddlers

Naples is notorious for its hawkers of high-tech goods, such as mobile phones and watches, being touted at incredible prices. No matter how careful the buyer is, the gadget purchased will turn out to be devoid of inner workings – or simply a piece of wood – once the box is opened. Other peddlers, however, may display jewellery, bags, scarves and such for sale at good prices – just be aware that none of it is worth a great deal.

9 Hair-raising Roads

Hairpin turns and narrow roads are hallmarks here, particularly along the Amalfi Coast. The motorways in and around Naples are badly maintained and confusing.

10 Looking Like a Lost Tourist

The secret to avoiding problems is the art of seeming to know what you're doing and where you're going. Don't carry cameras, bags and other paraphernalia all at once, and don't look too befuddled by chaos you may encounter. And avoid shadowy backstreets.

Left **Pharmacy sign** Right **Disabled toilets**

Top 10 Security & Health

1 Vaccinations

Despite its history of malaria, the plague and cholera outbreaks, the entire area is now as safe as anywhere else in the western world. No inoculations are required or recommended.

2 Prescriptions

Pharmacists in Italy serve as surrogate doctors. They are highly trained and can usually prescribe just the right thing, possibly homeopathic, once your symptoms are clear. Often, drugs that would require a prescription in your home country can be sold without one here. If you need to fill a specific prescription, it's important to know the actual chemical in question and not just its brand name, as that may be different in Italy.

3 Pharmacies

These are identified by a large red or green cross outside. They keep regular shop hours, but there will always be at least one in the area that is open outside normal hours. Look for the list posted next to the door of any *farmacia* for the schedule of off-hour openings around town.

4 Emergency Numbers

There are several national emergency numbers you can call, almost all toll-free, covering everything from crime, accident, fire, car breakdown, rescue and domestic emergencies of any sort *(see box)*.

5 English-Speaking Doctors

If you need an English-speaking doctor, contact your country's consulate in Naples. They have lists of doctors they can refer you to. *UK Consulate: Via dei Mille 40, Chiaia; 081 423 89 11; www.ukinitalia.it • US Consulate: Piazza della Repubblica, Mergellina; 081 583 81 11; www.usembassy.it • Canadian Consulate: Via G Carducci 29, Chiaia; 081 40 13 38*

6 Disabled Travellers

Getting around in a wheelchair in this area is a near impossibility without assistance. The larger museums and sights are making some headway at providing easier access, but the progress is slow. Disabled visitors will without a doubt require help from travelling companions at every stage of the journey.

7 Sun and Sea Protection

Temperatures in high summer can reach 30° C (86° F) and above, so it is important to wear a high factor sunscreen and a sunhat if walking around sightseeing – particularly children. Swimming in the Mediterranean is generally safe although lifeguards are rare.

8 Accidents

There are hospitals in each area that provide 24-hour emergency care. *Naples: Cardarelli 081 747 11 11 • Santobono: 081 220 57 97 • Capri: Capilupi: 081 838 12 05 • Ischia: Anna Rizzoli; 081 507 92 67 • Sorrento: Civico, 081 533 11 11*

9 Petty Crime

Pickpockets are not uncommon in crowded parts of Naples, particularly on public transport. Keep valuables tucked away in unreachable places. Losses or thefts should be reported to the nearest police station.

10 Serious Crime

Though petty thievery is part of the scene, violent crimes are quite rare in this society. Such things generally occur only in the underworld of organized crime far from regular tourist spots, in the seedier zones of suburbia.

Emergency Numbers

State Police 113

Carabinieri 112

Fire Brigade 115

Ambulance 118

Automobile Club d'Italia 803 116

Coastguard 1530

Mountain Rescue 1515

Left **Newspaper kiosk** Right **Post box**

Top 10 Banking & Communications

1 Exchange
Now that the euro is the coin of many realms, life is much easier for visitors to Europe, although the changeover has resulted in some price inflation, especially in Italy. Euro banknotes have the following denominations: 5, 10, 20, 50, 100, 200 and 500. Euro coins come in eight denominations: 1 euro, 2 euros, and 1, 2, 5, 10, 20 and 50 cents. Visitors from outside the euro zone should check the exchange rates at the time of travel.

2 Traveller's Cheques
If you're going to opt for this safety precaution, get your cheques directly in euros; that way you won't have to pay any commission to cash them and in some places you'll be able to use them as cash. Keep track of the serial numbers.

3 Cashpoints (ATMs)
For ready cash, this is the best option. Bank machines are everywhere and Italian banks charge no transaction fee; you'll only have your own bank's fee to pay for using a non-branch machine. If you withdraw the maximum each time (usually €300) the fee will probably be only about 1 per cent. But then be sure to keep your cash safe.

4 Credit Cards
Using your credit card is possible for almost everything in larger places. Only the smaller businesses will find it a problem, because of the 2–4 per cent commission that card companies charge them. Be aware that your own bank may charge you a 2 per cent currency conversion fee for every card purchase you make.

5 Wiring Money
This expensive, time-consuming process should be considered only as a last resort. You can have your bank send money to a bank in Italy, but you must organize things at the Italian end first. Then expect it to take an indeterminate number of days, with substantial charges at both ends of the process.

6 Post
For letters and postcards it's better to avoid the queues in post offices and buy *francobolli* (stamps) at *tabbachi* (tobacconists). Italian mail is improving but even *prioritaria* (priority) mail sometimes gets delayed. Mailboxes are red and have two slots – one *"per la città"* (local) and one for *"tutte le altre destinazioni"* (everywhere else). *Central post office: Piazza Matteotti, Toledo; 081 551 14 56; Open 8:15am–7pm Mon–Fri, 8:15am–noon Sat*

7 Phones
When dialling any number in Italy, you must include the area code and start with a zero. To call outside Italy, dial 00 then the country code, area code and number. Most public phones require a *scheda telefonica* (phonecard), available from *tabbachi*. *National Information: 12 • International Operator: 170 • International Information: 176*

8 Internet
Many hotels are geared up to allow you to use your laptop for accessing the Internet, and others provide the service at a foyer desk. Otherwise, Internet bars and cafés are common sights in every town and city, even in villages.

9 Newspapers
In the central kiosks you'll find a selection of international press. *USA Today* and the *International Herald Tribune* are generally available in tourist areas, as well as major British, German and French papers.

10 TV & Radio
Most up-market hotels will have satellite TV and the international news channels that come with it. Area radio includes a station from the nearby US base (106 and 107 FM) and some Italian stations play international chart hits.

Note: US mobile phones do not work in Italy but those from most other countries will.

Left **Villa Comunale** Right **Camp site**

TOP 10 Family and Budget Tips

1 Accommodation Breaks
Most accommodation options here welcome families. Italians love children and hotels often allow you to include any children up to a certain age – sometimes as high as the teens – at no extra charge, except perhaps a nominal fee for extra beds. The best budget option for families is a self-catering apartment.

2 Meals for Kids
Some restaurants in touristed areas have special kid's meals. Many will also obligingly prepare special foods for infants. There are also fast-food restaurants in the city that cater to kid's tastes, although it's the rare child who will not be thrilled with a pizza.

3 Shopping for Kids
There are shops galore that focus on what kids want, from toys to beach gear to gadgets. Such stuff is cheap enough – and cheaply made – so that you can simply leave it behind when it's time to go. A good range of fashions for children, toddlers and infants can also be found – some of it expensive.

4 Kids' Activities
Central Naples can be a difficult place for children, due to the almost complete lack of parks and other facilities. Local children, in the international view of things, would all appear to be street urchins to one degree or another. For wholesome fun, head for the parks – the Villa Comunale or Villa Floridiana are handiest. The castles, too, generally delight little ones, and, of course, Science City and Edenlandia, outside the city, are excellent *(see pp56–7)*.

5 Babysitting
Few hotels offer this service, so families should plan on non-stop togetherness when contemplating a trip to Naples and the province.

6 Picnicking
Given the wealth of natural beauty here, much of it now protected in parks and reserves, there are excellent picnicking opportunities. There are also wonderful markets and shops for stocking up on all that you'll need to put together a memorable repast, with settings and views to rival the best restaurants. Be sure to pick up any rubbish afterwards.

7 Self-Catering
Getting your own apartment can be an excellent option for an extended stay, not only for the money you'll save but also for the freedom you'll enjoy in doing the region entirely your own way. Prices can range from basic to high. Another advantage is that you will most probably get to know some locals *(see p132)*.
www.villaprato.it • www.ciaotour.it • www.vacation-rentals-europe.com

8 Camping
The best camp sites are good bargains and are located to the west of the city, handy for the archaeological areas of the Campi Flegrei. Be aware that the sea is not at its most inviting along this stretch of coast, but you will find spas and, from the port of Pozzuoli, you can take boats to the islands *(see p133)*.

9 Cutting Costs
All museums in Naples have free days and *ridotto* (reduced) admissions at all times for persons in certain categories. Another money-saver is to get the *Artecard* for Naples' cultural attractions from tourist offices. A cheaper way to get around the coast is by ferry rather than hydrofoil – half the price, but twice the time.

10 Off-Season
Low-season prices, from October to April (but not Christmas), can delight the budget-minded traveller. Note that on Capri and in many towns along the Amalfi Coast, however, some places close for the entire winter.

Keep an eye out for brochures, flyers and magazines with discount coupons to various attractions.

Left **Wheelchair lift** Right **Public convenience sign**

Top 10 Special Concerns

1 Disabled Travellers

Older buildings, which are often refurbished medieval structures, are usually entirely without facilities for the disabled – there are endless stairways and levels to contend with, sometimes even within a single room. The only good bet is to stay in the newest hotel you can find, where elevators will probably be big enough and bathroom sizes will all comply with EU laws. But double-check the details before booking anything. Even in major public buildings, there are almost always several steps.

2 Disabled Resources

Things are improving gradually, as more and more places try to upgrade in order to conform to EU standards. One of the most wheelchair-friendly places is Capri, where cars are few and ramps are everywhere since the main ways of getting luggage and people from one place to another is using electric carts. *Comune di Napoli: www.italiapertutti.it*

3 Senior Citizens

Seniors are entitled to discounts on transport fares and some entrance fees, but most offers apply to citizens of EU countries only. Older travellers should be prepared for a lot of walking, often in conditions of high temperature and humidity. In general, plan on taking it easy and limiting the scope of your day's activities.

4 Resources for Seniors

There are many educational programmes for seniors, operated by Elderhostel, Interhostel, and the Smithsonian, among others. These are carefully planned package tours or residential programmes that highlight aspects of the area. *www.elderhostel.org • www.learn.unh.edu/interhostel • SmithsonianJourneys.org*

5 Women Travellers

Compared to Northern Europe, attitudes here towards women can be quite macho. Still, women generally do not encounter excessive harassment and can travel alone without a problem. Naturally, exercise normal care, especially after dark. Don't stay around Naples' central train station if you are on your own.

6 Resources for Women

Your best resource for dealing with Lotharios is a firm *"no"* tinged with a touch of humour to make it clear you're not interested. There is a taxi service for single women and the driver will see you to your door. *Taxi Rosa: 081 552 5252 • www.consortaxi.it*

7 Student Travellers

There are plenty of options for students, including international hostels and discounts of various types if you have your student ID card. The Centro Turistico Studentesco will help with discount travel tickets. *CTS: Via Mezzocannone 25 • 081 552 7960 • www.cts.it • Open 9:30am–1:30pm, 2:30–6pm daily*

8 Public Conveniences

Public toilets are scarce, but bars are everywhere, and they are legally bound to let you use their facilities. You may need to tip an attendant in some places, such as at stations and in the toilets below the main piazza in Capri. Carrying toilet paper with you is always prudent.

9 Gay Travellers

Although this staunchly Catholic area is not noted for enlightened attitudes towards gays, there is generally little disapproval. Gay relations have never been outlawed in Italy.

10 Gay Areas

Most gay venues are usually straight clubs that sponsor special gay events or nights. There are also men's saunas, as well as cruising spots such as the Villa Comunale area after dark. *Bar B-Sauna: Via G Manna 14; 081 287 681*

Left **City break** Right **Coastal holidaymakers**

TOP 10 Accommodation Tips

1 Staying in Naples

Like all cities, the most convenient places to stay in Naples are in the centre of the city, making them accessible to all the main sights, but this can be quite an expensive option. For cheaper alternatives, the areas around Mergellina or the central station offer plenty of budget places to stay. Naples is also a good base for exploring Pompeii, Vesuvius and the islands *(see p131)*.

2 The Amalfi Coast

The coast to the south of Naples has long held a reputation for being expensive, with many luxurious hotels having taken advantage of the spectacular landscape. You will get what you pay for, however, as service and facilities are of a very high standard. Cheaper alternatives can be found in smaller towns, such as Praiano, but even Positano and Ravello offer some budget accommodation *(see p130)*.

3 The Sorrentine Peninsula

Again, Sorrento's reputation as a luxury resort is well founded, although there is no shortage of cheaper hotels – you will just find yourself further from the centre of things and with less breathtaking views. Towns such as Massa Lubrense and Castellamare di Stabia are better options if you are on a budget – and you will also encounter fewer crowds *(see p129)*.

4 Price Considerations

The area's hotels tend to be at the high end, but there are bargains to be found, even on Capri, that famously up-market magnet for the well-heeled. But you'll need to book well in advance for the best deals.

5 Making Reservations

Most hotels and even hostels now have Internet booking, but you should always follow up with a phone call and a fax. Italian hoteliers are famously slippery when it comes to confirmations and you could arrive to find that your reservation has been "lost". Double check, right up to the time of departure.

6 Finding Something on the Spot

In low season this may be possible, but in high season you are asking for trouble, especially in July and August when Italians themselves are on holiday. Be sure to book.

7 Tipping

Tipping is not the necessity here that it is in some countries, but if you found the service exemplary, leaving something for the staff is never amiss. You can leave a lump sum at the reception at checkout, or something in the room for the maids, or both. In most hotel restaurants, you will find a service charge of 15–20 per cent included on the bill.

8 Hidden Extras

Be sure to ask whether tax (IVA) is included in the rate you are quoted, and check to see if there are extra charges for such things as the fridge in your room and the use of the air-conditioning. Items from the minibar will, of course, cost much more than they are worth and telephone calls from your room may be exorbitant.

9 Travelling with Children

Most hotels are child-friendly and will give good price breaks on children sharing a room with their parents. Some make no charge and will provide an extra bed too. The best hotels may also provide a babysitter service.

10 Off the Beaten Track

You don't have to go very far from the tourist areas to find untouched corners where life hasn't changed in centuries. Here you'll find ancient traditions very much alive, as well as breathtaking scenery and fine cuisine, especially in the towns above the Amalfi Coast.

Above **Hotel Excelsior**

Price Categories

For a standard double room per night in high season (with breakfast if included), taxes and extra charges.

€	under €100
€€	€100-€150
€€€	€150-€200
€€€€	€200-€300
€€€€€	over €300

TOP 10 Naples' Luxury Hotels

1 Hotel Excelsior

This *belle époque* palazzo is the grande dame of Naples' plush hotels, and it has seen everyone from movie royalty to real monarchs pass through its elegant doors. Its situation is unsurpassed, with commanding views of the entire bay, Vesuvius and Castel dell'Ovo. *Via Partenope 48 • 081 764 01 11 • www.excelsior.it • Dis. access • €€€€€*

2 Grand Hotel Vesuvio

A 1950s reincarnation of the original 1882 grandeur, which was obliterated during World War II. It is consequently lacking in some of the charm of its neighbours, but is still the preferred lodging of many visiting VIPs. Again, its position is an enviable one, and the views from the upper floors are terrific. *Via Partenope 45 • 081 764 00 44 • www.vesuvio.it • Dis. access • €€€€€*

3 Grand Hotel Santa Lucia

Though more modest, this hotel has the most character of the three "grands" along the bay. It shares the same views and was renovated a few years ago. All the comforts you may require. *Via Partenope 46 • 081 764 06 66 • www.santalucia.it • Dis. access • €€€€*

4 Miramare

Built in 1914 as an aristocratic villa, this modernized hotel has retained its original Art Nouveau style. Located right on the bay, its lovely terrace and many rooms afford spectacular views. *Via Nazario Sauro 24 • Map N6 • 081 764 75 89 • www.hotelmiramare.com • Dis. access • €€€€*

5 Grand Hotel Parker's

This fine old hotel was a Grand Tour stopover and has recently been restored to its former glory, with antiques, chandeliers and original art. Be sure to visit the wonderful library, full of antiquarian books. There are two restaurants, one with postcard views from the roof garden. *Corso Vittorio Emanuele 135 • Map L4 • 081 761 24 74 • www.grandhotelparkers.com • Dis. access • €€€€€*

6 Hotel San Francesco al Monte

This atmospheric 16th-century Franciscan monastery opened as a hotel in 2002. All of the now-luxurious former monks' cells have views over the bay, and there's a garden restaurant with more vistas. Free shuttle-bus to the sights in the centre. *Corso Vittorio Emanuele 328, Vomero • Map K2 • 081 251 24 61 • www.hotelsanfrancesco.it • Dis. access • €€€€*

7 Britannique

A former *belle époque* private villa, it has been carefully converted and may have even more charm and style than it did originally. *Corso Vittorio Emanuele 133 • Map L4 • 081 761 41 45 • www.hotelbritannique.it • Dis. access • €€€*

8 Majestic

Simple, modern elegance and comfort are the keynotes here. The location is serene, only a short stroll from the Villa Comunale gardens and the waterfront. The area is also known for its fine restaurants. *Largo Vasto a Chiaia 68 • Map K5 • 081 41 65 00 • www.majestic.it • €€€€*

9 Paradiso

A Best Western chain hotel but Mediterranean in feel. Perched on Posillipo Hill, it's far from the city chaos and boasts a terrace restaurant with a stunning view of Vesuvius. *Via Catullo 11 • Map J2 • 081 761 41 65 • www.hotelparadisonapoli.it • Dis. access • €€€*

10 Starhotel Terminus

Given its location opposite the central station and its modern demeanour, this comfortable hotel caters mostly to corporate clients. A decent choice for those on the move. *Piazza Garibaldi 91 • Map R2 • 081 779 31 11 • Dis. access • €€€€*

***Note:** Unless otherwise stated, all hotels accept credit cards, have en-suite bathrooms and air conditioning*

Left **Hotel Canada** Right **Caravaggio**

TOP 10 Good-Value Naples Hotels

1 Parteno

Curiously, this establishment insists on calling itself a "bed and breakfast", but it more closely resembles an elegant boutique hotel. The rooms are beautiful, light and airy and the service most refined. ✆ *Lungomare Partenope 1 • Map L6 • 081 245 20 95 • www.parteno.it • €€*

2 Rex

Located by the sea in the famous Santa Lucia district, just around the corner from Naples' bastions of luxury, this hotel is full of period style. Most of the rooms have views and charming balconies. The decor, though simple, is comfortable, and breakfast is included and served in your room. ✆ *Via Palepoli 12 • Map N6 • 081 764 93 89 • www.hotel-rex.it • €€*

3 Chaia Hotel de Charme

This very special place actually consists of rooms in the restored palace of a Neapolitan *marchese*. It's appropriately located in Royal Naples so that you can indulge all of your aristocratic fantasies. The rooms are full of original furnishings and each is named after one of your host's noble ancestors. ✆ *Via Chaia 216 • Map M5 • 081 41 55 55 • www.hotelchiaia.it • Dis. access • €€*

4 Pinto-Storey

Dating from 1878 and redolent of bygone days, this hotel is very stylish, with Art Nouveau touches and an overall aura of gentility. It's in one of the nicest parts of town, not far from the Villa Comunale. Many rooms have great views of the bay, and air-conditioning is available at an extra charge. ✆ *Via G Martucci 72 • Map K5 • 081 68 12 60 • www.pintostorey.it • €€*

5 Hotel Canada

If you want to be in stylish Mergellina, with easy access to all the fun of the seafront social life, as well as hydrofoils to the islands, this is the choice. Rooms are homey, with caring touches here and there such as antiques and fresh flowers. ✆ *Via Mergellina 43 • Map K2 • 081 68 20 18 • www.sea-hotels.com • €€*

6 Caravaggio

Housed in a beautifully restored medieval building, in one of the most evocative parts of the old centre, this hotel exudes style. It's right behind the cathedral. ✆ *Piazza Cardinale Sisto Riario Sforza 157 • Map P2 • 081 211 00 66 • www.caravaggiohotel.it • €€€*

7 Neapolis

Up-to-the-minute services include a computer in your room with free Internet access. The location is handy to the old centre, and particularly to Piazza Bellini. The decor, though rather spartan, is comfortable. ✆ *Via Francesco del Giudice 13 • Map N2 • 081 44 20 81 • www.hotelneapolis.com • Dis. access • €€*

8 Toledo

Set in a restructured 17th-century *palazzo* in the earthy Spanish Quarter, this hotel is halfway between Royal Naples and the historic centre. It's convenient to every important monument and to all forms of public transport. ✆ *Via Montecalvario 15 • Map M4 • 081 40 68 71 • www.hoteltoledo.com • €€€*

9 Mercure Angoino

Part of an international chain and very modern, this is nevertheless a comfortable choice in Royal Naples. ✆ *Via A Depretis 123 • Map N4 • 081 552 95 00 • www.accorhotels.com • Dis. access • €€*

10 Charming International Hotel

This airport hotel is set in a redesigned 19th-century farmhouse, with every convenience, including a meeting room. ✆ *Viale Comandante Umberto Maddalena 35 • Map K1 • 081 231 10 04 • www.charminginternational.it • Dis. access • €€*

***Note:** Unless otherwise stated, all hotels accept credit cards, have en-suite bathrooms and air-conditioning*

Above **Bella Capri sign**

Price Categories

For a standard double room per night in high season (with breakfast if included), taxes and extra charges.

€	under €100
€€	€100-€150
€€€	€150-€200
€€€€	€200-€300
€€€€€	over €300

Top 10 Budget Hotels in Naples

1 Europeo

Modern and rather basic, this hotel is well located for checking out the university area as well as the ancient centre. They've made an effort to give a sense of style to all rooms and some are even decorated with wall frescoes. These rooms include breakfast, served on the roof terrace of the nearby Executive Hotel. *Via Mezzocannone 109 • Map P3 • 081 551 72 54 • www.sea-hotels.com • €*

2 Pensione Ruggiero

One of the more basic choices in town, but it's pleasant enough and very welcoming. Some rooms have air-conditioning, at an extra daily charge, and there's a garage nearby that offers a deal to guests. *Via G Martucci 72 • Map K5 • 081 761 24 60 • No en-suite bathrooms • €*

3 Bella Capri

Located right on the main port, with nicely furnished rooms on the sixth floor of a modern block, each room has great views of Mount Vesuvius and Capri from its own balcony. It's a pleasant walk to the Villa Comunale from here, and there are great restaurants in the area too. *Via G Melisurgo 4 • Map P4 • 081 552 94 94 • www.bellacapri.it • No air-conditioning • €*

4 Hostel of the Sun

This lively, international hostel also has a few private accommodations, and the price and location are certainly right. Set near the water, a stone's throw from Royal Naples and very convenient to the old centre. The atmosphere is friendly and the staff multilingual. *Via G Melisurgo 15 • Map N4 • 081 420 63 93 • www.hostelnapoli.com • No en-suite bathrooms • No air-conditioning • €*

5 Hotel des Artistes & Hostel

An elegant, friendly little place, just a few blocks from the Duomo in one direction and the Museo Archeologico in the other. Set in a period *palazzo* with a grand entrance and stairway. *Via Duomo 61 • Map P1 • 081 446 155 • www.hoteldesartistesnaples.it • No air-conditioning • €€*

6 Soggiorno Imperia

This simple place is homey and clean, offering kitchen and laundry facilities. No breakfast is served, but it's handy for popular Piazza Bellini, where there are great cafés, and to all the sights of the old centre. Be prepared to climb several flights of stairs, however. *Piazza Luigi Miraglia 386 • Map N2 • 081 45 93 47 • No air-conditioning • €*

7 Albergo Duomo

Perfectly located for doing the old centre, this is a basic place, but very well maintained and not without a certain charm. In this price range, you can't do better. Right across the street from the Duomo and just steps away from all the major sights of ancient Naples. *Via Duomo 228 • Map Q3 • 081 26 59 88 • No en-suite bathrooms • No air-conditioning • €*

8 Hostel-Pensione Mancini

As you come out of the main train station, walk straight across the huge square to the market. Or you can call them in advance and they'll come and meet you. *Via P S Mancini 33 • Map Q2 • 081 553 67 31 • www.hostelpensionemancini.com • No en-suite bathrooms • No air-conditioning • €*

9 Hotel Garibaldi

Newly refurbished and inside a quiet building on this busy square. *Via P S Mancini 11 • Map R2 • 081 563 06 56 • www.hotelgaribaldinapoli.com • No en-suite bathrooms • No air-conditioning • €*

10 Hotel Ginevra

Just outside the station, this *pensione* is an oasis of calm. *Via Genova 116 • Map R1 • 081 28 32 10/554 17 57 • No en-suite bathrooms • No air-conditioning • €*

Left **Grand Hotel Quisisana** Right **Hotel Caesar Augustus**

TOP 10 Capri Gems

1 Palatium

Standing above the port and painted a distinctive Pompeian red, this luxury hotel makes a conscious effort to recall the island's ancient heritage – in fact, this spot is where the Emperor Tiberius had one of his villas. There is a small beach for the use of guests as well as a seawater pool. Includes breakfast. *Via Marina Grande 225 • Map U1 • 081 838 41 11 • www.hotelpalatium.it • €€€€*

2 Grand Hotel Quisisana

This is the jewel in the crown of Capri exclusivity and has held that unrivalled position for decades for its opulence, attention to detail, as well as the sheer scale. Pools, gardens, restaurants, lounges, and private rooms are all serenely beautiful. There's also a beauty and fitness centre. *Via Camerelle 2 • Map U1 • 081 837 07 88 • www.quisi.com • €€€€€*

3 La Pazziella

The overall impression here is light-filled freshness, cool colours and serenity, yet it's just a few steps away from all the high-life in the *piazzetta* and the shops and restaurants. A wonderful place for a Capri sojourn. *Via P R Giuliani 4 • Map U1 • 081 837 00 44 • www.hotellapazziella.com • €€€€*

4 Villa Sarah

Located up towards Villa Jovis from the busy centre of Capri, this is a bucolic retreat. Its hillside position affords spectacular views of the island and the sea. The old villa has been beautifully converted, with antique details left just as they were, such as the old well in the patio. *Via Tiberio 3/A • Map U1 • 081 837 78 17 • www.villasarah.it • €€€*

5 Villa Krupp

Tucked away above the Gardens of Augustus, this whitewashed stone villa used to be Maxim Gorky's house. A more panoramic position would be hard to find, even on an island famed for its endless vistas. Beautifully decorated, in the light-suffused Capri way, with antique accents appropriate to its historic importance. *Viale Matteotti 12 • Map T2 • 081 837 03 62 • €€*

6 Weber Ambassador

With its commanding position overlooking this little port and beach, the Weber makes a perfect hideaway. The many terraces at several levels afford magnificent views of the famous I Faraglioni rocks, and the beach is just steps away from all this 4-star luxury. *Via Marina Piccola • Map T2 • 081 837 01 41 • www.hotelweber.com • €€€*

7 Capri Palace Hotel & Spa

After a recent makeover the comfort here is astounding. The beauty and spa programmes are more developed than elsewhere on the island, there's a large swimming pool and some suites have their own pools. *Via Capodimonte 2b • Map U1 • 081 978 01 11 • www.capri-palace.com • Dis. access • €€€€€*

8 Hotel Caesar Augustus

The Caesar Augustus takes its place among the finest accommodation options in the world. Its terrace dazzles with its position above the bay. *Via G Orlandi 4, Anacapri • Map T1 • 081 837 14 44 • www.caesar-augustus.com • Dis. access • €€€€*

9 Bellavista

Vine-covered walkways surround the main building, and the rooms are airy and well-appointed. *Via Orlandi 10, Anacapri • Map T1 • 081 837 14 63 • www.bellavistacapri.com • Dis. access • €€*

10 Villa Eva

This paradise, halfway to the Blue Grotto, has an array of accommodation, and a pool *(see p53)*. *Via La Fabbrica 8, Anacapri • Map S1 • 081 837 15 49 • www.villaeva.com • No air conditioning • €€*

Note: *Unless otherwise stated, all hotels accept credit cards, have en-suite bathrooms and air conditioning*

Above **Grand Hotel Excelsior Vittoria**

Price Categories

For a standard double room per night in high season (with breakfast if included), taxes and extra charges.

€	under €100
€€	€100-€150
€€€	€150-€200
€€€€	€200-€300
€€€€€	over €300

TOP 10 Sorrentine Peninsula Sojourns

1 Grand Hotel Excelsior Vittoria, Sorrento

Historic and utterly beautiful, with its clifftop position, extensive well-manicured gardens and grounds, and lavish public and private spaces. One of the world's best. *Piazza Tasso 34 • Map D5 • 081 807 10 44 • www.exvitt.it • Dis. access • €€€€€*

2 Imperial Hotel Tramontano, Sorrento

As the name states, this is another fabulous property, built on top of a Roman villa and frequented by the great and regal. Guests have included Romantic poets Shelley and Byron and the German writer Goethe. A pool, gardens, and striking panoramas render it as unforgettable today as it was in Grand Tour times. *Via Veneto 1 • Map D5 • 081 878 19 40 • www.tramontano.com • Dis. access • €€€€*

3 Bellevue Syrene, Sorrento

Built on the ruins of a 2nd-century BC Roman villa, this beautiful establishment carries the Roman theme forward with Pompeian decor in some rooms and even a Jacuzzi that has been made to resemble a Roman bath. *Via Marina Grande 1 • Map D5 • 081 878 10 24 • www.bellevue.it • Dis. access • €€€€*

4 La Tonnarella, Sorrento

With its clifftop setting and elegant interiors, this is an amazing find and fills up very fast, so you will need to book well in advance. Guests enjoy a pleasant private beach and a good restaurant in a wonderful glass-walled setting with panoramas of the bay. *Via Capo 31 • Map D5 • 081 878 11 53 • No air conditioning • €€*

5 Loreley et Londres, Sorrento

Quaint and a real bargain along this pricey coast. You get the views, the elevator to the beach, and some great cooking all at *pensione* prices. Though very basic, each room has a hair dryer, there are non smoking rooms upon request, free parking and good deals on half- or full-board plans. *Via Califano 2 • Map D5 • 081 807 31 87 • No air conditioning • €*

6 Nice, Sorrento

Small, simply furnished, and centrally located, this modest hotel is just a few blocks from the main square of Sorrento. *Corso Italia 257 • Map D5 • 081 878 16 50 • No air conditioning • €*

7 Hotel Capo La Gala, Vico Equense

Situated right on the seaside, in one of the most beautiful locations along the Sorrentine Coast, this lovely resort is hewn out of the living rock. There are only 18 guestrooms, each with a sea-view, and guests have access to sulphur baths, a private beach and a good restaurant. *Via Luigi Serio 8, Scrajo • Map D4 • 081 801 57 58 • www.capolagala.com • No air conditioning • €€€*

8 Grand Hotel La Medusa, Castellammare di Stabia

This grand country villa has an array of elegant touches, from terracotta vases adorning the gate, to the busts of Roman emperors, gardens, fountains and pool. Rooms are spacious and the dining is superb. *Via Passeggiata Archeologica 5 • Map E4 • 081 872 33 83 • www.lamedusahotel.com • Dis. access • €€€*

9 Hotel La Primavera, Massa Lubrense

This small restaurant-hotel, perched on a rocky spur, enjoys wonderful views and is surrounded by olive groves. *Via IV Novembre 3G • Map D5 • 081 878 91 25 • €*

10 Piccolo Paradiso, Massa Lubrense

A simple yet well laid-out hotel with a lovely pool and views. *Piazza Madonna della Lobra 5, Marina di Lobra • Map D5 • 081 808 95 34 • www.piccolo-paradiso.com • €*

Left **Villa Cimbrone gardens** Right **Villa Maria**

TOP 10 Amalfi Coast Stays

1 San Pietro, Positano

This 5-star hotel is 2 km (1 mile) east of Positano proper, but to the stellar clientele who are drawn to this marvellous place, it is well worth a bit of isolation. No fewer than 20 terraces, hewn out of the rock, feature individual accommodations with private balconies and Jacuzzis. A lift takes guests down to the foyer from the carpark above, and a second lift delivers you to the private beach far below. *Via Laurito 2 • Map E5 • 089 87 54 55 • www.ilsanpietro.it • €€€€€*

2 La Sirenuse, Positano

A palatial establishment that attracts well-heeled guests. It's all done up in signature Amalfi Coast style, with vibrant majolica tiles and lots of antiques. The pool is small, but there is a gym, and the hotel restaurant is renowned. *Via Cristoforo Colombo 30 • Map E5 • 089 87 50 66 • www.sirenuse.it • €€€€€*

3 Villa Franca, Positano

Given its clifftop location, there's a free minibus shuttle here. A wonderful choice, with incredible views and Mediterranean decor. Rooms have balconies and the rooftop pool is exquisite. *Viale Pasitea 318 • Map E5 • 089 87 56 55 • www.villafrancahotel.it • €€€€*

4 Luna Convento, Amalfi

This former convent has a unique position at one end of Amalfi, clinging to a cliff, with a fortified tower on the promontory that is now used for special events. Exquisite details and captivating colour schemes make it one of the most refined hotels in Italy. Cooking courses also held here. *Via Pantaleone Comite 33 • Map E5 • 089 87 10 02 • €€€€*

5 Hotel Cappuccini Convento, Amalfi

Gleaming white against the verdant cliff, this former monastery, dating from the 12th century, has been a hotel since 1821. Run by the same family ever since, they have maintained the Arabic-Norman architectural elements that make this place unique. Modern comforts are by no means overlooked either, and there are private gardens and beach. *Via Annunziatella 46 • Map E5 • 089 87 18 77 • www.hotelcappuccini.it • €€€€*

6 Palazzo Sasso, Ravello

Opened in 1997 in a 13th-century palace, the decor is a ravishing blend of Moorish and European elements. Incredible views and a fabulous restaurant. *Via S Giovanni del Toro 28 • Map E4 • 089 81 81 81 • www.palazzosasso.com • €€€€*

7 Hotel Palumbo & Palumbo Residence, Ravello

The 12th-century Palazzo Confalone has been converted into one of the finest hotels. Its architecture reveals Arabic and Oriental influences, while many of its columns are ancient Greek and Roman. The service is impeccable, while the views and the restaurant are unsurpassed. *Via S Giovanni del Toro 16 • Map E4 • 089 85 72 44 • www.hotel-palumbo.it • €€€€€*

8 Villa Cimbrone, Ravello

Inimitably fabulous and, after its 2003 sprucing up, more captivating than ever. Frescoed ceilings, priceless antiques and breathtaking gardens. *Via Sta Chiara 26 • Map E4 • 089 85 74 59 • www.villacimbrone.it • €€€€*

9 Villa Maria, Ravello

This atmospheric villa boasts one of the best restaurants in town. The vistas from the foyer are the stuff of dreams. *Via Sta Chiara 2 • Map E4 • 089 85 72 55 • www.villamaria.it/ • €€€*

10 Villa Amore, Ravello

You'll get the views here at a fraction of the price – and eat well on the garden terrace. *Via dei Fusco 5 • Map E4 • 089 85 71 35 • No air conditioning • €€*

***Note:** Unless otherwise stated, all hotels accept credit cards, have en-suite bathrooms and air conditioning*

Price Categories	
For a standard double room per night in high season (with breakfast if included), taxes and extra charges.	€ under €100
	€€ €100-€150
	€€€ €150-€200
	€€€€ €200-€300
	€€€€€ over €300

Above **Miramare e Castello**

Top 10 Island Charmers

1 Il Moresco Grand Hotel, Ischia

The neo-Moorish architecture, the spa and the careful service have made this hotel the meeting point of an international clientele. Situated in the most beautiful corner of the island, it is set in a green park surrounding a thermal pool, and is a few steps away from its own private beach. *Via E Gianturco 16, Ischia Porto • Map A4 • 081 98 13 55 • www.ilmoresco.it • €€€*

2 Miramare e Castello, Ischia

The premium rooms have balconies with bay vistas, but all accommodations are on the beach and in sight of the Castello Aragonese. Pluses include elegant public areas and lots of facilities – three pools, one with thermal water, a spa and beauty centre, and a private beach. *Via Pontano 5, Ischia Ponte • Map A4 • 081 99 13 33 • www.miramareecastello.it/ • €€€€*

3 Albergo Regina Isabella & Royal Sporting, Ischia

The hotel was at its peak in the 1950s. Somewhat faded, it's still sophisticated; overlooking the sea, facilities include a pool jutting out over the beach and spa services. *Piazza S Restituta 1, Lacco Ameno • Map A4 • 081 99 43 22 • www.reginaisabella.it • €€€€*

4 Hotel Terme Punta del Sole, Ischia

Situated in a splendid position in the heart of a quiet, flower-filled part of the island, this attractive hotel is not far away from sandy beaches and the famous Poseidon gardens. A tennis court and parking are conveniently located. *Piazza Maltese, Forio • Map A4 • 081 98 91 56 • www.hotelpuntadelsole.it • €€€*

5 Il Monastero, Ischia

This hotel occupies part of the monastery of the Castello itself. Consequently the rooms are quite spartan, but the views are prized. *Castello Aragonese, Ischia Ponte • Map A4 • 081 99 24 35 • www.castelloaragonese.it • No air conditioning • €€*

6 Villa Angelica, Ischia

A sunlit setting, Mediterranean architecture and hospitality is what greets you upon arrival. The sea is on your doorstep. *Via IV Novembre 28, Lacco Ameno • Map A4 • 081 99 45 24 • www.villaangelica.it • No air conditioning • €€*

7 Casa Conchiglia, Ischia

Mainly a restaurant, where you dine on a charming terrace with a port view, this modest villa also offers rooms for rent on the upper floor. Although close to the village centre, it's quiet enough and very friendly. *Via Chiaia delle Rose 3, Sant'Angelo • Map A4 • 081 99 92 70 • No air conditioning • €*

8 La Casa sul Mare, Procida

Housed in a building dating from 1700 and recently renovated, this hotel is at the foot of the acropolis of Terra Murata. Most rooms enjoy views of the picturesque fishing village. *Salita Castello 13, Corricella • Map B4 • 081 896 87 99 • www.lacasasulmare.it • €€€*

9 Casa Gentile Hotel, Procida

Glowing pink at one end of the port, this is a very attractive choice, reached on foot down the stone stairs worn away by the steps of generations of fishermen. The hotel has spacious rooms, and there's also a private pier where guests can anchor their boats. *Marina Corricella 88 • Map B4 • 081 896 77 99 • info@casagentile.it • No air conditioning • €*

10 Hotel Crescenzo, Procida

This little hotel is as much known for its fish restaurant as for its accommodation. Some rooms give directly onto the harbour. *Marina della Chiaollella 33 • Map B4 • 081 896 72 55 • www.hotelcrescenzo.it • €*

Left **Residence La Neffola** Right **La Fenice B&B**

TOP 10 Agriturismos, Villas & B&Bs

1 Agriturismo Il Casolare, Bacoli

The farmhouse here is actually situated in an evocative volcano that died out over 10,000 years ago. In this impressive scenery, time flows slowly, and you can appreciate the changing of the seasons. *Contrada Coste di Baia, Via Selvatico 12 • Map B3 • 081 523 51 93 • www.sibilla.net/ilcasolare • No credit cards • No air conditioning • €*

2 Agriturismo La Ginestra, Vico Equense

The farm's organically grown produce tempts most guests to sign on for half-board, but anyone can stop by for lunch or dinner as long as they telephone ahead. The farmhouse has airy rooms, many of which have good views down to the sea. *Via Tessa 2, Santa Maria del Castello • Map D4 • 081 802 32 11 • www.laginestra.org • No air conditioning • €*

3 Residence La Neffola, Sorrento

"Neffola" is the name of a fresh spring coming out of the rocks outside the town of Sorrento. The charming building here has been restored and is surrounded by beautiful gardens. *Via Capo 21 • Map D5 • 081 878 13 44 • www.nubedargento.com • No air conditioning • €*

4 Agriturismo Marecoccola, Sorrento

Amid countless paths to inaccessible beaches and the plantings of citrus trees, this farm has been run by the same family for over a century. Minimum 3-night stay. *Via Malacoccola 10 • Map D5 • 081 533 01 51 • www.fattoriamarecoccola.com • €€€*

5 Il Giardino di Vigliano, Massa Lubrense

The name originates from Roman times, as does the site, and the panorama inspires poets even to this day. Lemon groves abound here, their fragrance adding a sweet note to the air of total relaxation that is on offer here. *Località Villazzano • Map D5 • 081 533 98 23 • www.vigliano.org • No air conditioning • €€*

6 La Fenice B&B, Positano

The approach is up vine-covered steps to the white villa, where a shady terrace and many of the rooms enjoy memorable sea views. Furnishings are simple, but the hospitality doesn't get any more inviting. Stairs lead down to the seawater pool and Jacuzzi, all evocatively carved out of the living rock. *Via Marconi 4 • Map E5 • 089 87 55 13 • No credit cards • No air conditioning • €€*

7 Hotel Punta Chiarito, Ischia

Given its spectacular position, it's little wonder that guests refer to the place as a little paradise. It is surrounded by colourful and fragrant vegetation while a natural source of thermal water fills basins created with local stone. *Via Sorgeto 51, Forio • Map A4 • 081 90 81 02 • www.puntachiarito.it • €€€*

8 Il Vitigno, Ischia

This wonderfully earthy farm has a rustic rock-pool, a large terracotta tile terrace, and whitewashed elegance. It is also known in the area for its excellent cuisine. *Via Bocca 31, Forio • Map A4 • 081 99 83 07 • www.ilvitigno.com • No air conditioning • €*

9 My Home Your Home, Naples

This company has flats to rent either by the day or week in Naples. The website is easy to use; alternatively, stop by and talk to them in their office. *Via Duomo 276 • Map Q2 • 081 28 25 20 • www.myhomeyourhome.it • €€€*

10 Rent a Bed, Naples

For stays with private families this company offers range of choices and areas in Naples and on the coast. *www.rentabed.com*

Agriturismo *means working farms and estates that open their homes or grounds to guests. See www.agriturist.it for details.*

Price Categories

For a standard double room per night in high season (with breakfast if included), taxes and extra charges.

€	under €100
€€	€100-€150
€€€	€150-€200
€€€€	€200-€300
€€€€€	over €300

Above **Nube d'Argento Camping**

Top 10 Hostels and Camping

1 Ostello Mergellina, Naples

Not very central, but the district and the position are attractive in their own right. The facilities have been upgraded recently, rooms are well maintained and the staff is extremely friendly and helpful. Private double rooms are available and the evening meal is a real bargain for the area. *Salita della Grotta a Piedigrotta 23 • 081 761 23 46 • Dis. access • No credit cards • No air conditioning • €*

2 Casa del Pellegrino Hostel, Pompei

This former convent is certainly convenient for anyone visiting Pompeii. The building is in the low-rise style of ancient Rome, and, like a typical Pompeian house, it is built around a quiet inner courtyard. *Via Duca d'Aosta 4 • Map E4 • 081 850 86 44 • www.ostellionline.org • No credit cards • No air conditioning • €*

3 Il Gabbiano Hostel, Ischia

The island's youth hostel is generally packed in high season, but if you can get in, it's worth it. Perhaps its best feature is that it's located right above a lovely stretch of sand. *Via Provinciale Panza 182, Forio • Map A4 • 081 90 94 22 • No credit cards • No air conditioning • €*

4 Hostel delle Sirene, Sorrento

This self-proclaimed "VIP Backpacker" establishment is the best deal in town. Although short on views, it's convenient enough to everything of importance, and is located behind the train station. *Via degli Aranci 160 • Map D5 • 081 807 29 25 • www.hostel.it • No credit cards • No air conditioning • €*

5 Hostel A' Scalinatella, Atrani

In this family-run operation there are dormitory rooms, with private bath, and even apartments scattered all over town, up and down the staircases that serve as streets here. *Piazza Umberto I 5–6 • Map E5 • 089 87 14 92 • www.hostelscalinatella.com/ • No credit cards • No air conditioning • €*

6 Vulcano Solfatara Camping, Pozzuoli

Services here include a bar, a swimming pool, and even a restaurant. For doing the city of Naples, this is definitely the best camp site in the area, located conveniently near both a metro stop and the port of Pozzuoli for island trips in the area, as well. Independent bungalows are available, too. *Via Solfatara 161 • Map C3 • 081 526 74 13 • www.solfatara.it • No air conditioning • €*

7 Averno Camping, Pozzuoli

There are more facilities on offer here, including a tennis court, a pool, a Jacuzzi, a sauna, a bar, a restaurant, a gym and a disco. *Via Montenuovo Licola Patria 85, Arco Felice Lucrino • Map C3 • 081 804 26 66 • No en-suite bathrooms • No air conditioning • €*

8 Zeus Camping, Pompei

This verdant camp site is just steps away from the archaeological site. There are also bungalows for rent. Within the grounds you'll find a bar, a restaurant and shops. *Map E4 • 081 861 53 20 • www.campingzeus.it • Dis. access • No credit cards • No air conditioning • €*

9 Nube d'Argento Camping, Sorrento

This camp site enjoys views of Vesuvius. Facilities include pools and a restaurant. *Via Capo 21 • Map D5 • 081 878 13 44 • www.nubedargento.com • No credit cards • No en-suite bathrooms • No air conditioning • €*

10 Camping Mirage, Ischia

On a stretch of sandy beach, this is a great choice. *Via Marconi 37, Barano • Map A4 • 081 990 551 • www.campingmirage.it • No credit cards • No en-suite bathrooms • No air conditioning • €*

***Note:** Unless otherwise stated, all hotels accept credit cards, have en-suite bathrooms and air conditioning*

General Index

A

'a Taverna 'e zi Carmela (Naples) 87
Abbazia de San Michele Arcangelo (Procida) 101
accidents 120
Affaitati (Naples) 75
Africana (Marina di Praia) 103
Agriturismo Il Casolare (Bacoli) 132
Agriturismo La Ginestra (Vico Equense) 132
Agriturismo Marecoccola (Sorrento) 132
agriturismos 132
air travel 117
Aisha (Capri) 106
Al Faretto (Posillipo) 113
Al Gamberone (Pompeii) 93
Albergo Duomo (Naples) 127
Albergo Regina Isabella & Royal Sporting (Ischia) 131
Alberto al Mare (Ischia) 106
Alemanno, Pietro & Giovanni 23
Alfonso II, King 10
Alfonso V, King 10
Amalfi 100
  cafés and *gelaterie* 104
  hotels 130
  museums and galleries 39
  nightlife 103
  pizzerias 105
  restaurants 107
  shopping 102
Amalfi Coast 94–107
  cafés and *gelaterie* 104
  hiking 96
  hotels 124, 130
  map 94
  museums 101
  nightlife 103
  pizzerias 105
  restaurants 106–7
  shopping 102
  sights 100
  walks 49
ambulances 120
Anacapri 29
  cafés and *gelaterie* 104
  drives 49
  market 63
  museums 101
  nightlife 103
  restaurants 106
  shopping 102
  spas 51
Anfiteatro Cumano (Cuma) 113
Anfiteatro Flavio 110, 111
Aniello, Tommaso 35
L'Antica Pizzeria "da Michele" (Naples) 78
Antica Trattoria da Ciuffello (Pozzuoli) 111, 113
Aosta, Dukes of 18
Aquinas, St Thomas 45
L'Arco Antico (Amalfi) 102
Arco Naturale (Capri) 28
Area Archeologica de Santa Restituta (Ischia) 101
Aret' a' Palm (Naples) 86
Around Midnight (Naples) 86
L'Arte del Pulcinella (Naples) 75
Artis Domus (Sorrento) 103
artists 44–5
A.S. (Naples) 75
Associazione Scarlatti (Naples) 84
Astroni 112
Atignano (Naples) 63
ATMs 121
Atrani 100
  cafés and *gelaterie* 104
  hostels 133
  restaurants 107
Auden, W.H. 96
Augusteo (Naples) 84
Augustulus, Romulus 35
Aumm Aumm (Anacapri) 104
Averno Camping (Pozzuoli) 133

B

B&Bs 132
babysitting 122
Bacoli 112
  agriturismos 132
  restaurants 113
Baia 55, 110
  restaurants 113
banking 121
Bar degli Amorini (Ercolano) 93
Bar Anna (Paestum) 104
Bar Calise (Ischia) 104
Bar Ercolano (Sorrento) 104
Bar Mexico (Naples) 77
Bar Stany & Elio (Ischia) 104
Bar Tiberio (Capri) 104
Baracdero (Naples) 86
Bartolomeo, Fra' 19, 69
Bassolino, Antonio 35, 37
beaches 50–51
Beckett, Ernest 30
La Befana 64
beggars 119
Belisarius 34, 35
Bella Capri (Naples) 127
Bellavista (Capri) 128
Bellevue Syrene (Sorrento) 129
Bellini, Giovanni 18, 69
Bellini, Vincenzo 47, 70
Bellini (performing arts venue, Naples) 84
Bellini (restaurant, Naples) 79
Benevento 112
  restaurants 113
Benvenuta Primavera 65
Berevino (Naples) 77
Bernini, Pietro 13, 22, 40, 42
bicycles 118
Blue Grotto (Capri) 29, 53
boats 58, 59, 117, 118
Boccaccio, Giovanni 10, 30, 45
Bonaparte, Joseph 43
Borromini, Francesco 70
La Bottega della Ceramica (Naples) 85
Botticelli, Sandro 18, 44, 69
Bourbon dynasty 81, 111
Bourbon Street (Naples) 76
Bourdichon, Jean 22
Bowinkel (Naples) 85
Bracco (Naples) 84
La Brace (Praiano) 105
Bramante, Donato 13
Brancaccio, Cardinal Rinaldo 44
Brandi (Naples) 87
Britannique (Naples) 125
Buca di Bacco "da Serafina" (Capri) 106
buses 117, 118

C

cafés
  Amalfi Coast 104
  Spaccanapoli to Capodimonte 77
Caffarelli 47
Caffè Arabo (Naples) 77, 79
Caffè dell'Epoca (Naples) 77
Caffè Gambrinus (Naples) 87
Caffetteria Medina (Naples) 83, 87
Calcagno (Ercolano) 93
La Cambusa (Positano) 107
camping 122, 133
Camping Mirage (Ischia) 133
Cantina della Sapienza (Naples) 79
La Cantina del Sole (Naples) 79
Capasso (Naples) 79
Il Capitano (Positano) 107
Capo Posillipo 109
Capodanno 65
Capodimonte (Naples) 6, **18–19**, 38, 43, 69
Capri 7, **28–9**, 37, 95, 97
  beaches 50, 51
  cafés and *gelaterie* 104
  drives 49
  hidden attractions 55
  hotels 128
  museums 101
  nightlife 103
  pizzerias 105
  restaurants 106
  shopping 102
  souvenirs 63
  walks 49

Capri Palace Hotel & Spa (Capri) 51, 128
Capriccio (Ravello) 102
Caravaggio 19, 41, 44, 45, 69, 71
Caravaggio (Naples) 126
Carnevale 64
Carracci, Annibale 9
Carracciolo 38
cars 49, 117, 118
Casa Conchiglia (Ischia) 131
Casa Gentile Hotel (Procida) 131
Casa del Pellegrino Hostel (Pompeii) 133
La Casa sul Mare (Procida) 131
Casanova, Giacomo Girolamo 96
Casbah'r (Atrani) 104, 107
Caserta, drive to 49
Caserta Park (Naples) 43
Casertavecchia-San Leucio 113
cashpoints 121
Il Casolare da Tobia (Baia) 113
Castel Nuovo (Naples) 6, **10–11**, 81, 83
Castel dell'Ovo (Naples) 82
Castel Sant'Elmo (Naples) 21, 83
Castellammare di Stabia 51, 89
  hotels 129
  restaurants 93
Castello Aragonese (Ischia) 101
castrati 47, 82
catacombs 54–5
Cava de' Tirreni 100
Cavallini, Pietro 44, 74
caves 54
Ceramiche d'Arte (Ravello) 102
Ceramiche Solimene (Vietri sul Mare) 102
Certosa de San Giacomo (Capri) 101
Certosa di San Martino (Naples) 7, **20–23**, 40, 81
Cetara 51, 100
Chaia Hotel de Charme (Naples) 126
Lo Chalet (Naples) 87
Charcuterie Esposito (Naples) 75
Charles, Duke of Calabria 20
Charles I of Anjou 10, 12
Charles III, King 35, 36
  Capodimonte 18, 19, 43
  Paestum 32
  statue of 83
  Teatro San Carlo 82
  Vesuvian Villas 92
Charles V, Emperor 11, 36
Charming International Hotel (Naples) 126
children 56–7, 122, 124
Chiostro de San Francesco (Ravello) 30
Chocolat (Naples) 77
churches 40–41, 74, 119
Cimitero delle Fontanelle (Naples) 54
cinema 47
Città Sommersa (Baia) 55
climate 116
Codazzi 70
Colombo, Giacomo 20
Concerti al Tramonto, Villa San Michele (Anacapri) 65
La Conchiglia, Chiaia Beach (Procida) 106
Constantine, Emperor 13
consulates 116
Contatto (Naples) 86
Coralliuim (Anacapri) 102
Corenzio 40
Corradini 22
Correale di Terranova (Sorrento) 101
Corso Garibaldi (Naples) 63
credit cards 121
crime 119, 120
Criscuolo (Amalfi) 102
Croce, Benedetto 45
Crypta Neapolitana (Naples) 55
Il Cucciolo (Anacapri) 106
Culture Week 65
Cumae 37, 49, 55, 111, 113
cycling 118

D
Da Emilia (Sorrento) 107
Da Gemma (Capri) 105
Da Maria (Amalfi) 105
Da Michele 36 (Procida) 105
Da Pasquale, Sant'Angelo (Ischia) 105
Dal Cavaliere (Procida) 104
D'Angelo Santa Caterina Restaurant (Naples) 52
Daniele, Pino 46
Dante Alighieri 42
De Filippo, Eduardo 46
Decumano Maggiore (Naples) 48
Decumanus (Naples) 75
Depardieu, Gérard 47
Di Matteo (Naples) 78
Diocletian, Emperor 13, 111
disabled travellers 120, 123
Discoteca Valentino Pianobar (Ischia) 103
diving 58
doctors 120
Il Doge d'Amalfi (Amalfi) 104
Dolce & Amaro (Naples) 85
Domenichino 45
Don Alfonso 1890 (Sant'Agata sui Due Golfi) 107
Donatello 44, 74
Donizetti, Gaetano 47
Douglas, Norman 29
drinks 61
drives 49
Duomo (Naples) 6, **12–13**, 40, 69, 71
Duomo (Ravello) 31
Duomo (Scala) 31
Dürer, Albrecht 69

E
Edenlandia (Naples) 56
electricity 116
emergencies 120
Erchie 51
Ercolano 63, 93
Estate a Napoli 65
etiquette 119
Europeo (Naples) 127
Ex-ess (Naples) 86

F
Fanzago, Cosimo 42
I Faraglioni (Capri) 29
Farinelli 47
Farnese, Elisabetta 15
Farnese Collection 14, 15, 18, 38
Féfé (Bacoli) 113
La Fenice B&B (Positano) 132
Ferdinand I, King 52, 83
Ferdinand III, King 57
Ferdinand IV, King 15, 35
Ferragosto 65
Ferrante I, King 10, 11
ferries 117, 118
Festival delle Ville Vesuviane 65
festivals, religious 64–5
Fiera Antiquaria Napoletana (Naples) 63
Filangieri, Prince 38
films 47
fire services 120
Floridia, Lucia Migliaccio, Duchess of 52
Fontana, Domenico 8
Fontana dell'Immacolatella (Naples) 42
Fontana di Nettuna (Naples) 42
food 60–61
football 59
fountains 42–3
Francis of Assisi, St 23
Freezer (Naples) 86
Friggitoria-Pizzeria Giuliano (Naples) 78
funicular railways 57
Fusaro (Naples) 85

G
Il Gabbiano Hostel (Ischia) 133
La Galleria dell'Arte (Anacapri) 102
Galleria Toledo (Naples) 84
Galleria Umberto I (Naples) 82, 83
Gambrinus (Naples) 83
Garbo, Greta 30, 53

gardens *see* parks and gardens
Gardens of Augustus (Capri) 43
Garibaldi, Giuseppe 35
Gaudiosus, St 54
gay travellers 123
Gelateria Bilancione (Posillipo) 113
Gelateria della Scimmia (Naples) 77
gelaterie
Amalfi Coast 104
Spaccanapoli to Capodimonte 77
Gemito, Vincenzo 11, 19
Gennaro, San 6, 13, 54–5, 64, 69, 70, 111
Gentileschi, Artemisia 19, 45
Gesù Nuovo (Naples) 74
Giardini Poseidon (Ischia) 51
Il Giardino di Vigliano (Massa Lubrense) 132
Gide, André 95
Gigino Pizza al Metro (Vico Equense) 105
Giordano, Luca 9, 38, 45, 70
Giotto 10
Giuseppone a Mare (Posillipo) 113
Glykon of Athens 16
Gorky, Maxim 29
Gran Caffè Aragonese (Naples) 77
Grand Hotel Excelsior Vittoria (Sorrento) 129
Grand Hotel La Medusa (Castellammare di Stabia) 93, 129
Grand Hotel Parker's (Naples) 125
Grand Hotel Quisisana (Capri) 128
Grand Hotel Santa Lucia (Naples) 125
Grand Hotel Vesuvio (Naples) 125
Greeks 32–3, 36, 95
Green Grotto (Capri) 55
Greene, Graham 29, 95
Grieg, Edvard 30, 31
Grotelle Restaurant (Capri) 52
Guercino 9, 81
guglie (spires) 70
gyms 59

H
health 120
Herculaneum 7, **26–7**, 37, 89
hidden attractions 54–5
hiking 59, 96, 118
history 34–7
hospitals 120
Hostel-Pensione Mancini (Naples) 127
Hostel A' Scalinatella (Atrani) 133
Hostel delle Sirene (Sorrento) 133
Hostel of the Sun (Naples) 127
hostels 133
Hotel des Artistes & Hostel (Naples) 127
Hotel Caesar Augustus (Anacapri) 53, 128
Hotel Canada (Naples) 126
Hotel Capo La Gala (Vico Equense) 51, 129
Hotel Cappuccini Convento (Amalfi) 130
Hotel Crescenzo (Procida) 131
Hotel Excelsior (Naples) 125
Hotel Garibaldi (Naples) 27
Hotel Ginevra (Naples) 127
Hotel Palumbo & Palumbo Residence (Ravello) 130
Hotel La Primavera (Massa Lubrense) 129
Hotel Punta Chiarito (Ischia) 132
Hotel San Francesco al Monte (Naples) 125
Hotel Terme Punta del Sole (Ischia) 131
hotels 124–31
Amalfi Coast 124, 130
budget hotels in Naples 127
Capri 128
good-value Naples hotels 126
islands 131
luxury hotels in Naples 125
Sorrentine Peninsula 124, 129

I
icons of popular culture 46–7
L'Immacolata 65
Imperial Hotel Tramontano (Sorrento) 129
in-line skating 58
Innocent II, Pope 35
insurance 116
Internazionale Restaurant, Cafeteria & Bar (Pompeii) 93
Internet 116, 121
Internetbar (Naples) 77
Intra Moenia (Naples) 76, 77
Ischia 96, 97
beaches 50
drives 49
hostels and camping 133
hotels 131, 132
museums 39, 101
nightlife 103
places to eat 104–6
spas 51
walks 49
islands 94–7, 131

J
Joan I, Queen 35
Joan II, Queen 112
jogging 58
Justinian, Emperor 34

K
kayaking 58, 118
Kinky Bar (Naples) 76
Kukuwaya (Naples) 76

L
Lanfranco, Giovanni 20, 22, 70
Largo Corpo di Napoli 37
Lawrence, D.H. 95
Lazzaroni 46
Leucio (Casertavecchia-San Leucio) 113
Limonoro (Sorrento) 102
Lippi, Filippino 69
Liszt, Franz 95
Lombardi (Naples) 79
Lombardi a Santa Chiara (Naples) 78
Lontano da Dove (Naples) 76
Loreley et Londres (Sorrento) 129
Loren, Sophia 47
Lucullus 82
Luini, Bernardino 39
Luna Convento (Amalfi) 130
Lungomare (Naples) 48
Lysippus 14, 16

M
Madonna di Piedigrotta 65
Maffei (Naples) 85
Maggio di Monumenti 65
Magna Graecia 33, 34
Maiori 51, 100
Maison d'Art (Naples) 85
Majestic (Naples) 125
La Mammola (Torre del Greco) 93
Mantegna, Andrea 69
Marechiaro 52, 109
Maria Amalia, Queen 19, 92
Maria Carolina of Austria 35, 52
Marina di Equa 107
Marina di Furore 51
Marina Grande (Amalfi) 107
Marina Grande (Capri) 28, 49
Marina Piccola (Capri) 29, 57
Marina di Praia 51, 103
markets 63
Martini, Simone 18
Masaccio 44
Massa Lubrense 97, 129, 132
Maugham, Somerset 29
Mazzuoli, Giovanni 21
medicines 116, 120
Medrano, Antonio 18, 92
La Medusa (Procida) 106
Mellinoi (Naples) 75
Il Melograno (Ischia) 106
Mercadante (Naples) 84
Mercato dei Pulci (Poggioreale) 63

Mercure Angoino (Naples) 126
Metastasio, Pietro 47
Michelangelo 19, 69
Il Miglio d'Oro 92
Mimì alla Ferrovia (Naples) 79
Minori 51, 100, 101
Minuta 31
Miramare (Naples) 125
Miramare e Castello (Ischia) 131
Il Monastero (Ischia) 131
money 121
Monte di Pietà (Naples) 40
Monte Solaro (Capri) 29
Monteverdi, Claudio 82
Il Moresco Grand Hotel (Ischia) 131
La Mortella (Ischia)
motorcycles 117, 118
Murat, Joachim, King 35, 81
La Murrina (Naples) 85
Musei Interdipartimentali (Naples) 56
Museo Antiquarium Equano (Vico Equense) 101
Museo Archeologico (Paestum) 39
Museo Archeologico dei Campi Flegrei 110
Museo Archeologico Georges Vallet (Piano di Sorrento) 101
Museo Archeologico Nazionale (Naples) 6, **14–17**, 38, 69
Museo Archeologico di Pithecusae (Ischia) 39
Museo della Carta (Amalfi) 39
Museo Civico (Naples) 11
Museo Civico Filangieri (Naples) 38–9
Museo del Duomo (Ravello) 31
Museo Nazionale della Ceramica Duca di Martina (Naples) 39, 83
Museo di San Marino (Naples) 38
Museobottega della Tarsialignea (Sorrento) 39
museums and galleries 38–9, 101, 122
music 46
Music on the Rocks (Positano) 103
Mussolini, Benito 8
My Home Your Home (Naples) 132

N
Naccherino, Michelangelo 42
Napoli Sotterranea (Naples) 54
Napul'é (Naples) 75
Natale 65
nativity scenes 23, 46, 62
Neapolis (Naples) 126
Neapolis Festival 65
Negombo (Ischia) 51
Nerano 100
newspapers 121
Nice (Sorrento) 129
nightlife
Amalfi Coast 103
Spaccanapoli to Capodimonte 76
Toledo to Chiaia 86
La Ninfea (Pozzuoli) 113
Nonna Scepa (Paestum) 105
Notting Hill (Naples) 76
Nube d'Argento Camping (Sorrento) 133
Numero Due (Capri) 103
Nuovo Ristorante Anfiteatro (Pompeii) 93

O
Onassis, Jacqueline 29
opera 47, 82
Oplontis 26, 27, 89
Ordoñez, Bartolomé 71
Orio, Orazio de 21
Orto Botanico (Naples) 43, 70
Osmis (Naples) 75
Ospedale delle Bambole (Naples) 56
Ostello Mergellina (Naples) 133
Osteria da Tonino (Naples) 87
Otto Jazz (Naples) 86

P
Paestum 7, **32–3**, 37, 53, 95
cafés and *gelaterie* 104
drive to 49
museums and galleries 39
pizzerias 105
Palatium (Capri) 128
Palazzo Donn'Anna (Posillipo) 112
Palazzo Reale (Naples) 6, **8–9**, 81, 83
Palazzo Sasso (Ravello) 130
Palazzo dello Spagnolo (Naples) 71
Paradiso (Naples) 125
Parco Archeologico e Monumentale di Baia 110
Parco Termale Aphrodite Apollon (Ischia) 51
Parco Virgiliano (Naples) 43, 109
parks and gardens 43
Capodimonte (Naples) 43
Caserta Park (Naples) 43
Gardens of Augustus (Capri) 43
La Mortella (Ischia) 43
Orto Botanico (Naples) 43, 70
Palazzo Reale (Naples) 9
Parco Virgiliano (Naples) 43
Santi Marcellino e Festo Cloister (Naples) 43
parks and gardens (cont.)
Villa Cimbrone (Ravello) 43, 53
Villa Comunale (Naples) 43
Villa La Floridiana (Naples) 43
Parteno (Naples) 126
Parthenope 35
Pasqua (Easter) 64
pasticcerie 77
La Pazziella (Capri) 128
peddlers 119
Penna & Carta 1989 (Naples) 85
Pensione Ruggiero (Naples) 127
performing arts venues 84
Peter, St 41, 54
Petrarch 10, 45
Petronius 45
pharmacies 120
Phidias 14
philosophers 45
Philoxeno 17
Phlegrean Fields (Naples) 37, 49
phones 121
Piano di Sorrento 101
Piazza Bellini (Naples) 37, 42, 70, 71
Piazza Dante (Naples) 42
Piazza Duomo (Amalfi) 43
Piazza Duomo (Ravello) 43
Piazza Plebiscito (Naples) 42
Piazza Sannazzarro (Naples) 42
Piazza Sedile Dominova (Sorrento) 43
piazzas 42–3
Piazzetta, La (Capri) 42, 103
Piccolo Paradiso (Massa Lubrense) 129
pickpockets 119, 120
picnics 122
Pietrarsa Railway Museum 57
La Pignasecca (Naples) 63
Pinacoteca (Naples) 22–3
Pintauro (Naples) 87
Pinterré (Naples) 87
Pinto-Storey (Naples) 126
Pinturicchio 19
Pio Monte della Misericordia (Naples) 41, 71
Pit Bull Irish Pub (Procida) 103
Pizzafest 65
Il Pizzaiolo del Presidente (Naples) 78
Pizzeria Fortuna (Naples) 78
Pizzeria Sorbillo (Naples) 78
Pizzeria Vesi (Naples) 78
Pizzeria Vicolo della Neve (Salerno) 105
pizzerias 78, 105
Pizzofalcone (Naples) 37
Pliny the Elder 17
Pliny the Younger 27, 45
Poggioreale (Naples) 63

police 120
Politeama (Naples) 84
pollution 119
Polyclitus of Argos 14, 16
Pompeii 7, **24–7**, 37, 89
  hostels and camping 133
  restaurants 93
popular culture, icons of 46–7
Posillipo 108, 112
  beach 50
  market 63
  restaurants 113
Positano 100
  B&Bs 132
  beaches 51
  cafés and *gelaterie* 104
  drive to 49
  hidden attractions 55
  hotels 130
  nightlife 103
  restaurants 107
postal services 121
Pozzuoli 108, 109, 112
  camping 133
  restaurants 113
  walks 111
Praiano 100, 105
Praxiteles 14
presepi (nativity scenes) 23, 46, 62
Preti, Mattia 9
Il Principe (Pompeii) 93
Procida 96, 97
  beaches 50
  cafés and *gelaterie* 104
  hotels 131
  museums 101
  nightlife 103
  pizzerias 105
  restaurants 106
public toilets 123
Pulcinella 46, 64
Punta Carena (Capri) 29

R
radio 121
rail travel 57, 117, 118
Raphael 19, 69
Ravello 7, **30–31**, 95, 100
  drive to 49
  hotels 130
  Music Festival 31
  restaurants 107
  shopping 102
I Re di Napoli (Naples) 78, 87
regattas 59
Reggia di Caserta 111
Reggia di Portici 92
religious celebrations 64–5
Rembrandt 69
Rent a Bed (Naples) 132
Residence La Neffola (Sorrento) 132
Resina (Ercolano) 63
restaurants
  Amalfi Coast 106–7
restaurants (cont.)
  children in 122
  Posillipo, Pozzuoli and the North 113
  Spaccanapoli to Capodimonte 79
  Toledo to Chiaia 87
  Vesuvius and around 93
Rex (Naples) 126
Ribera, Jusepe 22, 38, 39, 45, 69
Rino Corcione (Naples) 85
Ristorante Suisse (Pompeii) 93
Ristorante Vittoria (Sorrento) 107
roads 119
Robert of Anjou 10, 45, 69
RocoCò (Amalfi) 103
Roger II, King 34
Romans 24–7, 36, 54–5
romantic spots 52–3
Rossellini, Roberto 47
Rossi, Francesco 47
Rossini, Gioacchino 47
Royal Naples 48, 80–87
Royal Porcelain Factory 19

S
sailing 58, 59
Salerno 97, 105
Salvatore (Ravello) 107
Salvatore Gargiulo (Sorrento) 102
San Domenico Maggiore (Naples) 74
San Francesco di Paola (Naples) 40, 81, 83
San Gaudioso Catacombs (Naples) 54
San Gennaro Catacombs (Naples) 54–5
San Giovanni 64
San Giovanni a Carbonara (Naples) 23, 71
San Giovanni al Toro (Ravello) 31
San Gregorio Armeno (Naples) 71, 74
San Lorenzo Maggiore (Naples) 37, 74
San Paolo Maggiore (Naples) 74
San Pasquale (Naples) 63
San Pietro (Positano) 130
San Pietro ad Aram (Naples) 41
San Pietro a Maiella (Naples) 74
San Severo Catacombs (Naples) 54
Sanakura (Naples) 76
Sancarluccio (Naples) 84
Sandalmakers (Capri) 102
Sanfelice, Ferdinando 71
Sangro, Raimondo di 70
Sanmartino 20, 22
Sannazaro (Naples) 84
Sannazaro, Jacopo 41
Sansevero Chapel (Naples) 70
Sant'Agata sui Due Golfi 107
Sant'Angelo a Nilo (Naples) 71, 74
Sant'Antonio (Sorrento) 105
Santi Apostoli (Naples) 70
Santa Chiara (Naples) 40, 69, 71
Santa Lucia (Naples) 41
Santi Marcellino e Festo Cloister (Naples) 43
Santa Maria delle Anime del Purgatorio ad Arco (Naples) 71, 74
Santa Maria Capuavetere 112
Santa Maria del Carmine (Naples) 64, 74
Santa Maria di Donnaregina Vecchia (Naples) 74
Santa Maria del Faro (Posillipo) 112
Santa Maria a Gradillo (Ravello) 31
Santa Maria Maggiore (Naples) 40–41
Santa Maria del Parto (Naples) 41
Santuario di San Gennaro (Pozzuoli) 112
Savardina "da Edoardo", La (Capri) 106
Scala 31
Scaturchio (Naples) 77
Science City (Posillipo) 56, 112
Lo Scoglio, Sant' Angelo (Ischia) 106
Scugnizzi 46
security 120
self-catering accommodation 122
senior citizens 123
shopping
  Amalfi Coast 102
  markets 63
  souvenirs 62–3
  Spaccanapoli to Capodimonte 75
  Toledo to Chiaia 85
Sibyl's Grotto (Cumae) 55
Siloe, Diego de 71
Simposium (Naples) 79
La Sirenuse (Positano) 130
S'move (Naples) 86
snorkelling 58
Soggiorno Imperia (Naples) 127
Solfatara (Pozzuoli) 57, 112
Solimena, Francesco 19, 20
Il Solitario (Anacapri) 106
Sorrentine Peninsula
  hotels 124, 129
  restaurants 107
  walks 49
Sorrento 96
  agriturismos 132

Sorrento (cont.)
beaches 50–51
cafés and *gelaterie* 104
drive to 49
hostels and camping 133
hotels 129
museums and galleries 39, 101
nightlife 103
pizzerias 105
restaurants 107
shopping 102
souvenirs 63
villas 132
Un Sorriso Integrale (Naples) 79
souvenirs 62–3
Spaccanapoli to Capodimonte (Naples) 48, 68–79
cafés, *gelaterie* and *pasticcerie* 77
churches 74
map 68
nightlife 76
pizzerias 78
restaurants 79
shopping 75
walks 71
Spadarino 81
Spadaro, Micco 22
Spartacus 35
spas 51
Spiaggia del Fornillo (Positano) 55
sports 58–9
Stabiae 26, 27
La Stanza del Gusto (Naples) 87
Stanzione 20, 23
Starhotel Terminus (Naples) 125
Steinbeck, John 94
Stokowski, Leopold 30
student travellers 123
Suetonius 45
sun protection 120
Superfly (Naples) 76
swimming 58, 120

T
La Tapas Bar (Naples) 76
Tasso, Torquato 45
Tattoo Records (Naples) 75
Taverna Anema e Core (Capri) 103
taxis 118
Teatro Gastronomico (Benevento) 113
Teatro Nuovo (Naples) 84
Teatro San Carlo (Naples) 47, 82, 83
telephones 121
television 121
Temple of "Ceres" (Paestum) 32
Temple of "Neptune" (Paestum) 32
tennis 59
Terme di Agnano 51
Terme Belliazzi (Ischia) 51
Terme di Cava Scura (Ischia) 51
Terme della Regina Isabella (Ischia) 51
Terme di Stabia (Castellammare di Stabia) 51
theft 119, 120
Tiberius, Emperor 28, 95
time zone 116
Tino di Camaino 22
tipping 124
Titian 9, 19, 44, 69
toilets 123
Toledo (Naples) 126
Toledo, Pedro de 36
Toledo to Chiaia (Naples) 80–87
map 80
nightlife 86
performing arts venues 84
restaurants 87
shopping 85
walks 83
La Tonnarella (Sorrento) 129
Torre Annunziata 89
Torre del Greco 92, 93
Torre del Saraceno (Marina di Equa) 107
Toscanini, Arturo 53
Totò 46
tourist offices 116
trains 57, 117, 118
Trajan, Emperor 112
Tramontano, Fratelli (Naples) 85
travel 117–18
traveller's cheques 121
La Trianon da Ciro (Naples) 78
Troisi, Massimo 47

U
Ulysses 94, 110
Underground (Anacapri) 103

V
vaccinations 120
Vanvittelli brothers 82, 92
La Vecchia Cantina (Naples) 79
Velluti, Gian Battista 47
Velvet Zone (Naples) 76
Verdi, Giuseppe 47
Vesuvian Villas 92
Vesuvius, Mount 25, 57
eruptions 34
Herculaneum 89
Pompeii 24, 27, 89
walks 49, 89
Vesuvius and around 88–93
map 88
restaurants 93
Via Anticaglia (Naples) 37
Via Krupp (Capri) 29
Via San Sebastiano (Naples) 75
Via Toledo (Naples) 48–9
Vibes (Naples) 86
Vico Equense 51, 96
agriturismos 132
hotels 129
museums 101
pizzerias 105
Vico, Giovanni Battista 45
Vidal, Gore 30, 53, 95
Vietri sul Mare 49, 100, 102
Villa Amore (Ravello) 107, 130
Villa Angelica (Ischia) 131
Villa Campolieto 92
Villa Cimbrone (Ravello) 30, 43, 53, 130
Villa Comunale (Naples) 43, 56, 82–3
Villa Eva (Capri) 53, 128
Villa Favorita 92
Villa La Floridiana (Naples) 43, 52
Villa Franca (Positano) 130
Villa Jovis (Capri) 28, 101
Villa Krupp (Capri) 128
Villa Maria (Ravello) 53, 130
Villa dei Papiri (Herculaneum) 26
Villa Romana (Minori) 101
Villa Rufolo (Ravello) 30, 65
Villa Ruggiero 92
Villa San Michele (Anacapri) 29, 65, 101
Villa Sarah (Capri) 128
Villa Verde (Capri) 105
villas 132
Virgil 45, 55, 82, 109
Virgilio Club (Naples) 86
visas 116
Il Vitigno (Ischia) 132
Vittorio Emanuele II, King 35
volcanoes 110
see also Vesuvius, Mount
Vulcano Solfatara Camping (Pozzuoli) 133

W
Wagner, Richard 30, 31, 95
walks 48–9, 118
hiking 59, 96, 118
Pozzuoli 111
Royal Naples 83
Spaccanapoli to Capodimonte 71
War Memorial Mausoleo (Posillipo) 112
weather 116
Weber Ambassador (Capri) 128
windsurfing 58
wine 61
women travellers 123
writers 45

X, Y, Z
Zagara, La (Positano) 104
Zeus Camping (Pompeii) 133
Zi Caterina (Pompeii) 93

Acknowledgements

Main Contributor
American-born Jeffrey Kennedy now lives mainly in Italy and Spain. A graduate of Stanford University, he divides his time between producing, acting and writing. He is the co-author of *Top 10 Rome* and the author of the Top 10 guides to *Mallorca, Miami and the Keys, San Francisco* and *Andalucía*.

Produced by Sargasso Media Ltd, London

Editorial Director
Zoë Ross
Art Editor
Clare Thorpe
Picture Research
Helen Stallion
Proofreader
Stewart J Wild
Indexer
Hilary Bird

Photographer
Demetrio Carrasco
Illustrator
chrisorr.com

FOR DORLING KINDERSLEY
Publisher
Douglas Amrine
Managing Art Editor
Marisa Renzullo
Senior Cartographic Editor
Casper Morris
DTP
Jason Little
Production
Shane Higgins
DK Picture Researcher
Romaine Werblow

Maps
Tom Coulson, Martin Darlison (Encompass Graphics Ltd), Fabio Ratti Editoria. Source data for the Amalfi Coast map derived from Netmaps www.netmaps.es

Picture Credits
t-top; tc-top centre; tr-top right; cla-centre left above; ca-centre above; cra-centre right above; cl-centre left; c-centre; cr-centre right; clb-centre left below; cb-centre below; crb-centre right below; bl-below left; bc-below centre; br-below right.

Every effort has been made to trace the copyright holders, and we apologize in advance for any unintentional omissions. We would be pleased to insert the appropriate acknowledgements in any subsequent edition of this publication.

The publishers would like to thank the following

individuals, companies, and picture libraries for permission to reproduce their photographs:

Grazia Neri/Toty Ruggieri: 56c; Corbis: 1, 14t, 14cb, 14b, 14–15, 15c, 15t, 15b, 20–21, 24–5, 26tl, 27tr, 27b, 31t, 34tl, 34tr, 34b, 35tl, 35r, 36tl, 36tr, 36c, 37b, 46tl, 46tr, 46c, 47t, 47r, 51r, 58tl, 58b, 65r, 75tl, 82b, 85tl, 85tr, 90–91, 93tl

Dipino Ravello Ceramics Shop: 102tr

Getty Images: 59; Grazia Neri:45tr, 64tl, 72–3, /Foto Mairani: 4–5, 7b, 8cl, 9t, 23c, 33t, 33c, 33b, 68tr, 95b, 111, /Francesco Vignali: 8–9, 32tr, /Guglielmo Mairani: 23b, /Stefano Cellai: 40tl, 42tl, 42b

Hotel Canada: 126tl; Hotel Caravaggio: 126tr; Hotel Miremare e Castello: 50tl, 97r, 31t

Il Dagherrotipo/Andrea Getuli: 32–3, 55t, /Giorgio Oddi: 94tr, /Giovanni Rinaldi: 18tl; 80tl; /Marzia Giacobbe: 94c, /Stefano Occhibelli: 43r, 62tl, 108c; Index/Alberti: 10tl, 65b, /Barbieri: 6ct, 8b, 9c, /Pizzi: 19t

Luciano Pedicini; 16tl, 16tc, 16tr, 16b, 17t, 17b, 22tl, 22tr, 30–31, 38b, 54b

Scala: 6br, 9b, 11t, 11b, 18c, 18–19, 18b, 19c, 19b, 22b, 38tl, 38tr, 44tl, 44b, 45tl.

Jacket
Front: Corbis: Mimmo Jodice ca; DK Picture Library: John Heseltine cb, b; Ian O'Leary t; Getty Images:Taxi/David Noton main image. Back: DK Picture Library: John Heseltine l, c; Museo Archeologico di Napoli r.

Phrase Book

In an Emergency

Help!	**Aiuto!**	*eye-yoo-toh*
Stop!	**Fermate!**	*fair-mah-teh*
Call a doctor.	**Chiama un medico**	*kee-ah-mah oon meh-dee-koh*
Call an ambulance.	**Chiama un' ambulanza**	*kee-ah-mah oon am-boo-lan-tsa*
Call the police.	**Chiama la polizia**	*kee-ah-mah lah pol-ee-tsee-ah*
Call the fire brigade.	**Chiama i pompieri**	*kee-ah-mah ee pom-pee-air-ee*

Communication Essentials

Yes/No	**Si/No**	*see/noh*
Please	**Per favore**	*pair fah-vor-eh*
Thank you	**Grazie**	*grah-tsee-eh*
Excuse me	**Mi scusi**	*mee skoo-zee*
Hello	**Buon giorno**	*bwon jor-noh*
Goodbye	**Arrivederci**	*ah-ree-veh-dair-chee*
Good evening	**Buona sera**	*bwon-ah sair-ah*
What?	**Quale?**	*kwah-leh?*
When?	**Quando?**	*kwan-doh?*
Why?	**Perchè?**	*pair-keh?*
Where?	**Dove?**	*doh-veh?*

Useful Phrases

How are you?	**Come sta?**	*koh-meh stah?*
Very well.	**Molto bene.**	*moll-toh beh-neh*
Pleased to meet you.	**Piacere di conoscerla.**	*pee-ah-chair-eh dee-coh-noh-shair-lah*
That's fine.	**Va bene.**	*va beh-neh*
Where is/are ...?	**Dov'è/ Dove sono ...?**	*dov-eh/doveh soh-noh?*
How do I get to ...?	**Come faccio per arrivare a ...?**	*koh-meh fah-choh pair arri-var-eh ah..?*
Do you speak English?	**Parla inglese?**	*par-lah een-gleh-zeh?*
I don't understand.	**Non capisco.**	*non ka-pee-skoh*
I'm sorry.	**Mi dispiace.**	*mee dee-spee-ah-cheh*

Shopping

How much does this cost?	**Quant'è, per favore?**	*kwan-teh pair fah-vor-eh?*
I would like ...	**Vorrei ...**	*vor-ray*
Do you have ...?	**Avete ...?**	*ah-veh-teh.. ?*
Do you take credit cards?	**Accettate carte di credito?**	*ah-chet-tah-teh kar-teh dee creh-dee-toh?*
What time do you open/close?	**A che ora apre/ chiude?**	*ah keh or-ah ah-preh/kee-oo-deh?*
this one	**questo**	*kweh-stoh*
that one	**quello**	*kwell-oh*
expensive	**caro**	*kar-oh*
cheap	**a buon prezzo**	*ah bwon pret-soh*
size, clothes	**la taglia**	*lah tah-lee-ah*
size, shoes	**il numero**	*eel noo-mair-oh*
white	**bianco**	*bee-ang-koh*
black	**nero**	*neh-roh*
red	**rosso**	*ross-oh*
yellow	**giallo**	*jal-loh*
green	**verde**	*vair-deh*
blue	**blu**	*bloo*

Types of Shop

bakery	**il forno /il panificio**	*eel forn-oh /eel pan-ee-fee-choh*
bank	**la banca**	*lah bang-kah*
bookshop	**la libreria**	*lah lee-breh-ree-ah*
cake shop	**la pasticceria**	*lah pas-tee-chair-ee-ah*
chemist	**la farmacia**	*lah far-mah-chee-ah*
delicatessen	**la salumeria**	*lah sah-loo-meh-ree-ah*
department store	**il grande magazzino**	*eel gran-deh mag-gad-zee-noh*
grocery	**alimentari**	*ah-lee-men-tah-ree*
hairdresser	**il parrucchiere**	*eel par-oo-kee-air-eh*
ice cream parlour	**la gelateria**	*lah jel-lah-tair-ree-ah*
market	**il mercato**	*eel mair-kah-toh*
newsstand	**l'edicola**	*leh-dee-koh-lah*
post office	**l'ufficio postale**	*loo-fee-choh pos-tah-leh*
supermarket	**il supermercato**	*eel su-pair-mair-kah-toh*
tobacconist	**il tabaccaio**	*eel tah-bak-eye-oh*
travel agency	**l'agenzia di viaggi**	*lah-jen-tsee-ah dee vee-ad-jee*

Sightseeing

art gallery	**la pinacoteca**	*lah peena-koh-teh-kah*
bus stop	**la fermata dell'autobus**	*lah fair-mah-tah dell ow-toh-boos*
church	**la chiesa**	*lah kee-eh-zah*
closed for holidays	**chiuso per le ferie**	*kee-oo-zoh pair leh fair-ee-eh*
garden	**il giardino**	*eel jar-dee-no*
museum	**il museo**	*eel moo-zeh-oh*
railway station	**la stazione**	*lah stah-tsee-oh-neh*
tourist information	**l'ufficio di turismo**	*loo-fee-choh dee too-ree-smoh*

Staying in a Hotel

Do you have any vacant rooms?	**Avete camere libere?**	*ah-veh-teh kah-mair-eh lee-bair-eh?*
double room	**una camera doppia**	*oona kah-mair-ah doh-pee-ah*
with double bed	**con letto matrimoniale**	*kon let-toh mah-tree-moh-nee-ah-leh*
twin room	**una camera con due letti**	*oona kah-mair-ah kon doo-eh let-tee*
single room	**una camera singola**	*oona kah-mair-ah sing-goh-lah*
room with a bath, shower	**una camera con bagno, con doccia**	*oona kah-mair-ah kon ban-yoh, kon dot-chah*
I have a reservation.	**Ho fatto una prenotazione.**	*oh fat-toh oona preh-noh-tah-tsee-oh-neh*